TOSCA

LIBRETTO DI V·SARDOU
L·ILLICA - G·GIACOSA
MUSICA DI G·PUCCINI
G·RICORDI & C· EDITORI

Giacomo Puccini

by Conrad Wilson

Φ

In Memoriam Alexander Gibson

Phaidon Press Limited
Regent's Wharf
All Saints Street
London N1 9PA

First published 1997
© 1997 Phaidon Press Limited

ISBN 0 7148 3291 X

A CIP catalogue record for this book is
available from the British Library

Printed in Singapore

Frontispiece, the cover
design for the libretto of
Tosca published by the
Casa Ricordi

Contents

Preface

Puccini, even if we refuse to admit it, is the composer through whom most of us learn to love opera. That many of us thereafter learn to hate Puccini seems an act of ingratitude, but it is a fate that childhood heroes all too often suffer. Later, with luck, some of us grow to love Puccini all over again, this time usually for good. Being one of the reconverted, I have been happy to write this book, discovering in the process that I love not only the music but also – something I thought less likely – the man.

Not all composers, after all, are as attractive as their works, and Puccini the man, it had always seemed to me, was the price we had to pay for his music. But this, as I increasingly found, was a blinkered judgement of him. Creative artists, being what they are, possess priorities that can make them seem insensitive to other people's feelings. They can be vain, mean, cruel, cowardly, impatient, two-faced and treacherous. Puccini, in these respects, was no more saintly than many others. But he was not insensitive. His personal pleasures – expensive cars, speed boats, the shooting of water fowl, the pursuit of performances of his own (and other people's) operas around the world – were largely hedonistic. For the failure or misery of his marriage he was probably more than half to blame. He was lucky, though some would prefer to say selfish, to have had so many ways of escape.

But the more you learn about him, the more you recognize and perhaps understand the anxieties from which he suffered so severely – above all the fear of failure that is many a creative artist's nightmare. Even some of the best of Puccini's operas were badly received at the outset, and the première of *Madama Butterfly* was a public humiliation from which he found it hard to recover. A deep sense of uncertainty prompted him to tinker with many of his works, though whether he improved them in the process remains a moot point. Yet he possessed one infallible gift for which he has been – and continues to be – both loved and criticized. That was the gift of melody. The ability to write a good tune may be no guarantee of greatness; but the ability to write a good tune and then to place it, seemingly effortlessly, in the context of a work that is beautifully crafted, unerringly paced. and precisely coloured is a token of genius that should never be underestimated.

Puccini, although he composed only twelve operas, had this quality in abundance, and it is what gives his music undiminishing appeal. His characters live, and they transfigure the plays and books from which most of them were drawn. Without Puccini's musical flair, nobody would care very much today about Murger's Mimi or Belasco's Butterfly. There were aspects of Puccini – his inner melancholy, his marital problems, his tendency to proclaim 'Oh horror!' or 'My life is ended!' at times of sometimes no more than minor stress, and finally the tortured grotesquerie of his death – that can make him seem like a character out of one of his own operas.

To say, as many people do, that he did not aim very high, or at any rate not as high as Wagner or Verdi, may be true. But he aimed high enough. His contribution to operatic history was considerable. And I have found, in writing this book, that he has become a friend, surely something which all but the most spiteful biographers must hope for.

In writing this book, I feel all too aware that I am trailing in the footsteps of Mosco Carner, whose classic and comprehensive study of the composer has been an invaluable source of information. Yet in the end I have found myself disagreeing with some of his psychological assessments, and with his failure to rate certain works as highly as I believe they deserve. Far from finding fault with them – as many Puccini specialists are prone to do – I have gained a special affection for them, the way one sometimes does for a composer's so-called 'mistakes'. This is not, therefore, a book that employs Puccini's best works as clubs with which to batter the weaker ones. Il trittico, it seems to me, is not improved by the omission – as some would prefer – of sweet, sentimental Suor Angelica. Far from being an embarrassment, the quiet yet dark-edged centrepiece of the triptych is surely a vital component of it, a Puccini himself well knew. Far from being immature, his early opera Edgar is a work of striking originality and personality, as Toscanini recognized when he conduced excerpts from it at Puccini's funeral.

Many people seem to have hang-ups about Puccini, and the conversations I have had with fellow critics, academics, friends and opera lovers while writing this book have reminded me of the fact. He still has the power to disturb – always a good thing in a composer. In the darkness of the theatre, his operas can still, if the performances are good enough, bring tears to our eyes. He himself would doubtless consider that to be a fair tribute to his abilities. It was, after all, one of the things he set out to do, and which, a century after the première of *La bohème*, his music continues to do with ease.

Conrad Wilson
Edinburgh, Scotland/Introbio, Italy, 1996

Introduction

A distinguished English critic once observed that opera houses need
Puccini the way farms need dung. The quip was less insulting than it
sounded. Without *La bohème, Tosca* and *Madama Butterfly* as a
permanent part of their repertoire, most opera companies would be in
penury. These works, along with the occasional *Turandot, Manon
Lescaut,* and *La fanciulla del West,* are the fertilizer that enables the
music of composers less popular than Puccini to survive today's
financial rigours.

At the New York Metropolitan, where he was adored and fêted
during his lifetime, Puccini still fills seats: one in three performances,
it was recently calculated, is of a work by him. In London, Covent
Garden's original (and much loved) 1899 production of *La bohème* ran,
with few gaps, for seventy years, and generations of distinguished
singers starred in it. New opera houses, as far apart as Sydney and
Lyon, have seen the need to add Puccini without delay to their
repertoire. When the Los Angeles Music Center Opera was founded
in 1985, *Madama Butterfly* was one of the first three operas it staged. In
Glasgow, *Tosca* and *Madama Butterfly* have become Scottish Opera's
longest-running successes, their quality sustained by perceptive
productions, by a willingness to rethink without distorting the
composer's intentions, by good young casts, and, until his recent
death, by the loving conducting of Sir Alexander Gibson.

The alert young Flemish Opera, too, has been looking at Puccini
afresh, assembling a substantial modern Puccini cycle in Antwerp and
Ghent, unified by the mind of one perceptive director, Robert Carsen,
in a way that respects both the composer's genius and the audience's
intelligence. A browse through a single issue of *Opera* magazine in
1995 revealed reviews of a *Tosca* in Milwaukee (with Sherrill Milnes as
Scarpia), a *Tosca* and *Turandot* in Sydney, a *Bohème* in Montreal, a
Trittico in Brussels, and another *Trittico* in Hamburg with Harry

Kupfer, the controversial Wagnerian, as its unlikely director. There
were announcements in the same issue of a new *Turandot* in London,
a *Madama Butterfly* in Munich, a *Bohème* in Vienna, a *Tosca* in
Helsinki, and a *Trittico* in Tunbridge Wells. Italy itself recently listed
seventeen productions of *Bohème*, six of *Tosca*, three each of *Madama
Butterfly* and *Il tabarro*, two each of *La rondine*, *Gianni Schicchi* and
Manon Lescaut, and one each of *Turandot*, *La fanciulla del West*, *Suor
Angelica*, and *Le villi*. Only *Edgar* was absent.

Many more examples could be cited of Puccini's continuing
popularity. At times of prosperity, major companies will invite Franco
Zeffirelli to stage a new production of *La bohème* with Luciano
Pavarotti as Rodolfo and six hundred choristers in the twenty-minute
Café Momus scene. At times of adventure, they will try to persuade
Carlos Kleiber to conduct *Bohème*, or Peter Sellars to update *Madama
Butterfly*. At times of crisis, they can always fall back on Puccini and be
thankful that they can do a *Bohème*, any sort of *Bohème*, on the cheap.

The theory, however, that Puccini's works are basically mere
money-spinners – not too expensive to perform, not too time-
consuming to rehearse – has been rightly, and increasingly,
questioned. His principal roles require subtle singers. His orchestral
parts need to be rehearsed exhaustively and played with the utmost
finesse. Puccini himself, who kept a close eye on productions of his
operas, and travelled the world to see them, grumbled that Covent
Garden was content to supply star singers but was too mean to
provide a convincingly integrated staging. Perhaps, or perhaps not, he
would say the same today. No operas, in fact, are less in need of stars -
unless, perhaps, they are young stars – than Puccini's. All his heroes
and heroines are youthful, and nothing looks less realistic than a
mature, bosomy Tosca when the whole point of the role is that she
should be as young, brave, and loyal as Beethoven's operatic heroine,
Leonore.

Today it is no longer good enough to describe Puccini simply as a
composer who 'brings in the audience'. Yet it is his very popularity
that irks certain critics who insist that his works, like those of Richard
Strauss, get in the way of operatic progress, occupying long stretches
of the season that could be more usefully devoted to other things. The
operatic repertoire, as Joseph Kerman brutally put it in *Opera as
Drama*, is 'still clogged with relics from the general period 1890 to

1914'. If Puccini were a more challenging composer – rather than someone who 'borrowed and bowdlerised up-to-date techniques for his own conservative ends' – critics of Kerman's sort might object less strenuously. But because they regard him as Italian trash, 'false through and through', they are prepared to proclaim that between Verdi and Puccini, just as between Wagner and Strauss, 'lies the decisive gulf between art and sensationalism'.

From the start, avows Kerman, 'Puccini and Strauss revealed a coarseness of sensitivity and a deep cynicism towards true dramatic values, characteristics that simply deepened as their techniques grew more and more impressive.' Judged from that standpoint, Puccini's last opera, *Turandot*, was not the best of his works but the worst, a dreadful example of 'café-music banality'.

Yet when composers arouse critics in this way, it does not necessarily mean that they are bad composers. Wagner himself – and Brahms and Berlioz – have been thus attacked, and frequently, for reasons that ultimately boil down to the purely personal. All we have learned is that these critics simply dislike these composers, and have nothing constructive to say about their works. As Alan Walker states in his *Anatomy of Music Criticism*, our method of judgment is merely a litmus test. You dip a critic into music and see what colour he turns. The composer remains as he was.

Puccini's musical soft spot for 'little women', and what is traditionally said to be his coarsely sadistic treatment of them, has certainly turned some critics purple. Yet although he was clearly not averse to subjects with a dash of sadism, it would be wrong to describe his operas as sensationalist. There was far more to them than that, and as the period in which he wrote them recedes into history we are becoming increasingly aware of the fact. His ability to adopt up-to-date international techniques to his own purposes was not a matter of 'borrowing and bowdlerising', but of adjusting them creatively to his innate Italian lyricism. It is true that a more rigorously intellectual Italian composer would not be accused of compromise as Puccini has been. But Luigi Nono and Luigi Dallapiccola, to name but two, have paid the penalty for seeking a more didactic twentieth-century operatic destiny: in the years after their deaths, their audiences have run dry.

Puccini, on the other hand, sought subjects which would be popular and which he knew he could enhance with his music. He

spent an enormous amount of time searching for the right plot and
the right libretto, and his efforts were rewarded. That his operas still live
more than seventy years after his death is indicative of Puccini's
significance. Though his musical sound effects are often described as too
'calculated', he wrote with an emotional tenderness for which he has not
been given full credit. 'They say that emotionalism is a sign of
weakness,' he once remarked, 'but I like to be weak.' It was, in Puccini's
case, the sign of an enduringly successful Italian opera composer.

Weakness, of course, can take many forms. Puccini's weaknesses
were for a certain sort of story or play, for heroines who, as he put it,
were 'losers', for a certain sort of sadness, for music that could play
(and still plays) on the heart strings, and for a personal lifestyle which,
in the end, was his own undoing. Indeed, in the way he lived, Puccini
might be called the first 'modern' composer. He was a dandy who
drove fast cars, had his own chauffeur, bought speed boats, shot game,
visited spas, toured the Alps, enjoyed train journeys, was ceaselessly
photographed, composed his operas for singers whose voices were
regularly recorded, and died – as a chain smoker – of throat cancer.

But although he liked to dress flamboyantly, and enjoyed taking
curtain calls after successful performances, Puccini generally valued his
privacy. To walk round Lucca, his Tuscan hometown, is to be
reminded that - whatever his music may say to the contrary – he was a
man of some severity. There is no Puccini industry in Lucca to
compare with the Mozart industry in Salzburg. The people of this
quietly beautiful walled city do not crudely and publicly exploit his
memory (some say cynically that they are too mean to do so). Books
and scores can be bought from the open-air stalls near the theatre. But
Puccini cakes, chocolates, and souvenirs – or, perhaps more to the
point, Puccini pasta, olive oil, and match boxes – are not a priority.
The first thing to strike you about the place is the dignity with which
he is remembered. The kitsch that so horrendously mars Salzburg is
conspicuously missing.

The composer's boyhood home in the narrow, shadowy via di
Poggio – a substantial first-floor flat overlooking the daily *passeggiata*
to and from the Piazza San Michele – has been transformed into a
museum of the most serious kind. There are no false notes. A
selection of manuscripts, a piano, a gramophone, a picture of
Madama Butterfly dating from the year of its première, one of

Puccini's fur-collared overcoats, samples of his hand-writing (very untidy) and that of his publisher Giulio Ricordi (very neat) are what you see. The two main rooms have beamed ceilings, with brickwork above. Although there is piped music, usually *La bohème*, it is discreet. The atmosphere is cool and respectful. You do not learn much of the composer's personality, which is exactly how he would have wished it. Across the road the Piccolo Albergo Puccini – the only hotel in town to pay nominal tribute to him – is similarly simple, discreet, inexpensive, and a good place to stay if you want a bit of peace. The nearby Ristorante Puccini is in keeping. An old building, with a smartly modernized bright yellow interior, it shuns sentimental memorabilia and serves imaginative dishes, and is again reassuringly inexpensive. Crostini Puccini – little pieces of toast with Tuscan toppings – are a characteristically low-keyed tribute to the composer.

Puccini's own place to eat and drink, however, was the Caffè Caselli, which opened in 1858 (the year of his birth) and which has survived in the via Fillungo. Even if you did not know its Puccini connections beforehand, you would need only to pause outside its window to guess it to be an authentic piece of Puccinian Lucca. It is a café of a sort fast disappearing in Italy, although a few good examples can still be found in Rome, Milan, Turin, Trieste and Naples.

Nobody yet has transformed the Caffè Caselli into a Burgy or a McDonald's. Good coffee, breakfast rolls, sweet Italian-style brioches, small cakes, ice-cream, and *aperitivi* are still served from different sections of its long and stylish nineteenth-century counter. You can eat and drink standing up or, much more expensively, sitting down at the back of the café – which gives you, for your money, time to look around you, and note the 1986 etching of Puccini (the tenth of a set of a hundred) and the plaque that tells of the café's cultural history, and those from the musical, literary and figurative arts worlds who once frequented it, including not only Puccini but Catalani, Giacosa, Pascoli and Mascagni. Today a baby grand piano and a microphone sit beneath the plaque, but the old tiled floor, the octagonal coffee tables, the smoky ceiling, the mirrors and alcoves, the back rooms and courtyard speak eloquently of an earlier era.

From his villa at Torre del Lago, where he composed most of his operas, Puccini regularly drove the short distance to his friend Alfredo Caselli's café in Lucca, which at the time must have had something of the character of a smoking club. But Torre del Lago itself – now named Torre del Lago Puccini in tribute to its most distinguished resident – in no way vulgarizes the memory of the man who, the villagers once complained, composed 'harlots' music'. The long, straight main street, some distance back from the lake, is plain to the point of being characterless. Only its name, the viale Puccini, and its offshoots, the via Tosca, via Turandot, via Gianni Schicchi and so forth, show it to be somewhere different from countless other Italian villages of its sort in the area.

On the lakeside, small souvenir shops sell good posters and postcards, rather than nasty trinkets, and the Butterfly Restaurant, a few steps from Puccini's villa, is by no means as ominous as it sounds. Indeed it serves quite serious food (even under such names as Tortelli Butterfly) at uninflated prices, and the red Michelin guide recommends *sarda*, a type of mackerel, as a house speciality. The open-air theatre, where the Festival Pucciniano has been held each summer for more than forty years, has space for 3500 people, yet does not dwarf the lake front or seem to shout 'Look at me!' This is not Bayreuth any more than it is Salzburg.

Out of season, the place still exudes the peace for which Puccini loved it. In the distance, across Lake Massaciuccoli, the gleam of traffic on the busy A12 to Florence is a sight he did not know, and (despite his predilection for motoring) would have hated. But the lake itself looks undefiled and the statue of the composer, complete with familiar hat and overcoat, stands at ease, puffing a fateful cigarette. True, visited on a quiet February day, the place can look a little melancholy, as if it were the inspirational source of the Puccini 'melodic droop', a feature of all his operas. The villa, too, when not open to the public, looks shuttered and gloomy, hemmed in by a heavy fence, as if still mourning the death of the owner whose body lies within. It is then that the friendliness of the Butterfly Restaurant is welcome, before one takes the bus back to Viareggio, the nearby seaside resort where, in a different villa between beach and parkland, Puccini spent his last years.

I

*They say that emotionalism is a sign of weak-
ness, but I like to be weak.*

Giacomo Puccini

Youth 1858–85

As music often runs in families, it should be of no surprise that
Giacomo Puccini was of strong musical stock. But in his maturity he
looked more like the latest in a long line of bank managers than
someone capable of composing *La bohème*. Nor in adolescence could
his face be said to have burned with the zeal of a young Giuseppe
Verdi. He did not sport a romantic beard. His expression in
photographs tended to be rather blank. His hooded eye-lids and
unsmiling mouth gave him an impassive, disdainful, even mean
appearance. His parents, as pictures of them reveal, possessed the same
appraising look, and his mother the same haughty expression,
suggesting that she would brook no nonsense from inferiors. Puccini's
origins may have been humble, but – so her grim face seemed to say –
they were not peasants, and woe betide anyone who said so. Indeed
her gifted son, the fifth of seven children (only two of whom were
male), was to prove the last practising member of a long and
accomplished line of musicians.

Five generations of Puccinis played an active role – as composers,
organists and choirmasters – in one or another of Lucca's exquisite
churches. The first Giacomo Puccini (1712–81) – the composer's great-
great-grandfather – was himself a prodigious composer, writing
seventeen Masses, ten Te Deums, twenty-two Motets, twelve
Lamentations, and, perhaps more significantly in view of the
achievements of his future namesake, a series of *Tasche*, a type of
political serenata which, along with virgin olive oil, became something
of a Lucca speciality.

Born in the village of Celle, among groves of larches and oaks in
the hills beyond the city (and where local wines were of notable
quality), Great-Great-Grandfather Puccini was clearly no ordinary
rustic musician. He had the initiative, for example, to journey a
hundred miles to Bologna, one of Italy's most celebrated musical
centres at the time, in order to make contact with Padre Martini, its
leading music teacher. To befriend, as he did, someone who had

The first Giacomo Puccini
(1712–81) was the
composer's great-great-
grandfather. Founder of the
musical dynasty of Puccinis,
he was an organist, choirmaster and industrious
composer of church music.

encouraged the boy Mozart, and to sustain a substantial
correspondence with him later, clearly served this ambitious young
Tuscan in good stead. As Mozart's father had remarked, two words
from Padre Martini were worth more than the warmest
recommendation from a king. As a result, by the age of twenty-seven,
the first of the musical Puccinis had firmly established himself in
Lucca as organist and choirmaster at the handsome San Martino
Cathedral, a building famous throughout Europe. His diaries, which
he wrote scrupulously until shortly before his death, have provided a
valuable commentary on all aspects of life in Lucca.

Far from being hilltop peasants, the Puccinis were to become a
musical dynasty more durable than the Mozarts and the Couperins, if
not quite the equal of the Bachs. The senior Giacomo Puccini's son,
Antonio, followed his father's footsteps to Bologna, and thereafter in
Lucca he held much the same sort of appointments. Antonio Puccini's
son, Domenico, likewise headed for Bologna but then diversified by
going to Naples and becoming a pupil of Giovanni Paisiello –
composer of a by no means negligible *Il barbiere di Siviglia* that
predated Rossini's comedy by almost forty years. But before long he

Giacomo Puccini's mother
Albina, *above*, and father
Michele, *right*. Although
Puccini bore a facial
resemblance to each of them,
he inherited, in particular, his
mother's hooded eyes.

too returned to Lucca, to produce church music of what has been been described as 'astounding' theatricality. He was certainly theatrical enough to have composed six operas and conducted Domenica Cimarosa's comedy, *Il matrimonio segreto*, at the local court theatre.

Paisiello left an indelible mark on the Puccini family, and his influence was there to stay. Domenico Puccini's son, Michele, confirmed this fact. Following his father's example, Michele went first to Bologna, then to Naples, where – Paisiello by then being dead – his teachers were the even more influential Donizetti and Mercadante. These were big names in the Italian opera world, even if Mercadante's reputation has now declined. Michele Puccini was soon doing what was expected of him: composing operas and church music, in addition to his duties as teacher and organist at San Martino Cathedral. But for the Puccini dynasty he did one thing more. At the age of forty-five, having already sired four daughters, he became the father of Giacomo Antonio Domenico Michele Secondo Maria Puccini, future composer of *La bohème, Tosca, Madama Butterfly*, and nine other operas.

Bearing, as he did, the Christian names of so many generations of Puccinis, it seemed appropriate that Giacomo would amount to more than their sum total. He was the genius towards whom the Puccini family had been aspiring for more than one hundred and fifty years. Sadly, Michele Puccini did not live to savour his son's triumph. Never strong, he died when Giacomo was five. Nor did he know that he would have a second son, born after his death, who would also be named Michele. And although young Michele proved to have musical hopes, it soon became plain that genius was not destined to strike the Puccini family twice. His talents, overshadowed by those of his elder brother, failed to burgeon. After studying at Milan Conservatory he emigrated to South America, where he died at the age of twenty-six, in what seem to have been mysterious circumstances.

But musical genius rarely repeats itself within a single family. In finally producing Giacomo, the Puccinis seemed in a sense to have fulfilled themselves in the same curious way as the Mozart genius petered out after the death of Wolfgang Amadeus. These were not isolated examples. The sons of Johann Sebastian Bach, for all their talent, were not the calibre of their father. The Wagners, still going strong, have diversified their abilities into other aspects of theatre. Handel, Haydn, Beethoven, Schubert, Rossini, Bellini, Brahms,

Chopin, Tchaikovsky, Musorgsky, Ravel, Bruckner – to name but twelve – died childless. No doubt a study of the psychology of genius could propose some reasons for this phenomenon.

When Giacomo Puccini died he took not only his own genius with him but five generations' worth of music as well. The organs of Lucca's churches no longer have members of the Puccini family to play them. Giacomo's son Antonio (1886–1946) was not a musician but a civil engineer. His granddaughter Simonetta, born in 1929, has kept the family flame burning in various ways as an editor of Puccini memorabilia and exhibition organizer.

Puccini's muse flowered more slowly than Mozart's, perhaps because he did not have a father to tend it. Michele's early death clearly deprived the boy of the sort of attention that Leopold Mozart gave young Wolfgang, although Giacomo reported that he did have memories of his father. His mother was however the dominant – very dominant – influence on his boyhood. An Italian 'mamma' of some determination, she ensured that he got the musical education he deserved. And when money later ran short she wrote to the Queen of Italy, among others, for support.

It was his mother's brother, Uncle Fortunato, who taught Puccini music after his father's death, and who encouraged him to sing as a treble not only in the cathedral choir but in that of the gleaming 'wedding-cake' church of San Michele, a few steps from the Puccini home. It is not always mentioned that there was music on the maternal side of the family, but Fortunato Magi was the proof of it. Magi, who also taught Alfredo Catalani, another Lucca-born opera composer, was director of the local Istituto Musicale Pacini. It has now been renamed the Boccherini Institute, in tribute to yet another composer who hailed from Lucca (unlike Giovanni Pacini). When Uncle Fortunato retired from his post, young Giacomo, by then sixteen, became a pupil of his successor, Carlo Angeloni, a religious composer of some repute.

As a place in which to hear and study music, Lucca was evidently not such a backwater as it has been made out to be, although Boccherini escaped from it fast. Quite apart from its useful geographical position between Pisa and Florence – along with the fact that (by the time Puccini was old enough to care) Bologna, Milan and Rome were all within increasingly easy reach – it had its own strong

Puccini's birthplace in the narrow via di Poggio, Lucca, a few steps away from the church of San Michele, where the future composer was baptized and sang as a boy chorister. The Puccini home at No. 30 is now a museum.

theatrical life, both sung and spoken. It was in Lucca that Puccini first saw a play by Sardou (whose *Tosca* he would later transform into an opera), first gained a general knowledge of French drama, and first explored the music of Debussy, Schoenberg, Strauss and Stravinsky. All this was to be of great benefit to him in the course of his career.

Yet as a child Puccini was no prodigy. So far as is known, he did not tease his father, Mozart-fashion, by creeping to the keyboard and playing an unresolved chord in the middle of the night, thus forcing his tormented parent to rise and resolve it. He was not a brilliant instrumentalist. He did not sing like Rossini. He did not compose prophetic pieces to rival those of the ten-year-old Sibelius, whose *Drops of Water*, a pizzicato duet for violin and cello, pointed the way to his later musical output, or those of Prokofiev, whose *Little Dogs* (so named 'because they bite so') similarly anticipated his adult style. Puccini's musical taste-buds developed in an entirely (and, as we shall see, characteristically) mercenary way. His father – and this, significantly, was one of Puccini's few memories of him – used to take him to church, where he would place small coins on the keys of the organ, so as to interest his young son in the instrument. Puccini, eager to grab them, found himself inadvertently pressing the notes. Surprisingly enough – considering the inducement – he never became much of an organist. In fact he showed a preference for bird-catching, an activity he pursued, with increasing zeal, into adulthood. There was a point, indeed, when one suspects that Puccini might not have developed into a composer at all. His musical studies progressed in a routine sort of way, and his teenage ability to act as deputy organist in Lucca's plethora of churches in no way challenged the capability of many another reasonably musical boy.

To keep himself in cigarettes – the fact that he chain-smoked from boyhood provided early evidence that he was destined to die from throat cancer – he found another modest source of income, which was to play the piano in the bars and brothels in the narrow streets behind the cathedral, in the same way as the otherwise strait-laced Brahms had done in Hamburg. Brahms, however, had ambitions to be a great pianist. For Puccini it was just a job of work.

Playing concertos and sonatas, let alone composing them, was never to be his scene. For Puccini the piano was purely a tool, useful (as he subsequently discovered) in his work as a composer – like

Wagner and many others he liked to write at the keyboard – and
pleasant to play in convivial company, but not much more than that.
Whether, as is sometimes said, he eked out his boyhood income by
stealing and selling organ pipes seems never to have been confirmed.
But the story that the theft of pipes, by him or someone else, forced
him to make changes in the harmony of the music he played in
church carries the ring of truth. From an early age, he was nothing if
not a practical musician.

Teaching the organ to a local tailor, and writing short pieces for
him, again showed that Puccini was alert to all the possibilities of
earning a modest income through music. Like the organ pieces he
improvised in church, this was small beer but it pointed the way. His
church music, it is said, possessed an unseemly sunniness, even when
it was meant to be funereal, and he was not averse to substituting folk
tunes for chorales. Even then he sensed there to be life beyond the
organ loft, and the chance to take home the scores of some of Verdi's
operas filled him with a deep desire to see *Aida*, which, when he was
eighteen, finally reached Pisa, five years after its Cairo première.

Verdi, exact contemporary of Wagner in Germany (though they
never met each other), was by then well established in musical terms
as Italy's voice of political freedom. As successor to Rossini, Bellini and
Donizetti, he bestrode the Italian operatic scene unchallenged, as
Puccini was well aware. Of all Italian operatic composers, Verdi was
the one who really mattered to him. The chance to see *Aida* in a
neighbouring city was therefore irresistible. Consequently, with a
couple of friends – and this is a story well vouched for – he set out
from Lucca on foot, a round trip of about thirty miles, and reckoned
the effort amply justified.

Even if, as some cynically suspect, part of the journey was made by
public transport, it nevertheless showed a degree of musical
fanaticism. Indeed, if there could be said to have been a turning point
in Puccini's formative years, this was surely it. Before *Aida*, his career
could have gone in any direction. After hearing it, he knew that he
would become a composer of operas. 'When I heard *Aida* in Pisa,' he
later remarked, 'I felt that a musical window had opened for me.'
Wise after the event, he subsequently added: 'Almighty God touched
me with his little finger and told me to write for the theatre – mind,
only the theatre.'

Lucca's handsomely asymmetrical San Martino Cathedral, where the young Puccini played the organ. To increase his meagre income, he became a pianist in the bars and brothels in the narrow streeets behind the cathedral.

How he would establish himself as a composer of operas – he had no contacts nor any operatic experience – seems not to have worried him. Though God this time gave him no hints, Puccini had the desire, and just enough music in his bones, to make it seem possible. Like many another hopeful Italian opera composer of the period, he might have got nowhere. But the five generations of music within him suddenly came to the fore. His first notable work was not an opera but quite a sizeable orchestral *Preludio Sinfonico*, or Symphonic Prelude, written soon after the *Aida* experience, while he was still eighteen. Its self-assurance, and a melancholy turn of melody that later came to be recognized as the characteristic Puccini 'droop', have ensured it an occasional performance, usually by part-time or amateur orchestras more prepared to undertake such things than professional organizations.

But Riccardo Chailly and the Berlin Radio Symphony Orchestra have recorded it, along with other juvenilia, sympathetically enough to provide a real impression of its qualities. It is not without crudity, but as an Opus 1 – even though Puccini did not employ opus numbers – its qualities are not to be gainsaid. It opens, without any sort of preamble, with a somewhat baldly-stated melody that nevertheless has a prayer-like character. It was the fountainhead of other musical prayers that Puccini later incorporated in his operas. Individual fingerprints, indeed, are everywhere – in the way the music mounts to its sonorous climax, in the plaintive resumption of the prayer, in the gentle ending – and one is left with the impression that here is a prelude crying out for an opera.

Next came a patriotic cantata, *I figli d'Italia bella* ('The Sons of Beautiful Italy'), which Puccini entered, unsuccessfully, for a competition in 1878. His manuscript, not for the last time, was returned to him as illegible. Good musical script was never his strong suit, but performers and publishers bore more patiently with this shortcoming once they recognized that their efforts were worthwhile.

Many of his prentice pieces are preserved in the Puccini house in Lucca, in order that people may see for themselves what they looked like. Lucca, though not a leading Italian operatic centre, encouraged him as best it could. A Motet and Credo were composed by him, also in 1878, for the annual Feast of San Paolino, the city's patron saint and the inventor, it is said, of the church bell. They were first performed, appropriately enough, on the saint's day on 12 July, when the bells were duly rung.

Later, Puccini expanded the two movements into a five-movement Mass for Four Voices and Orchestra, which likewise won a performance in Lucca. Though the local press praised its 'noble' ideas, this was not yet enough to win it a publisher. Not until 1951, after it had been renamed the *Messa di Gloria* in tribute to the exhilarating march that forms its Gloria movement, did it do so. Today it possesses sufficient curiosity value to enjoy an occasional public performance or recording, and the fact that it was originally considered 'a little theatrical' (in the manner of so much nineteenth-century Italian church music) has clearly done it no harm.

Puccini, himself recognizing its theatricality, later purloined its Kyrie for use in his first full-length opera, *Edgar*, and its Agnus Dei reappears as a madrigal in his first mature opera, *Manon Lescaut*. Like Berlioz before him, Puccini prudently salvaged from his juvenilia anything that seemed good and worth recycling. Just as Berlioz's *Symphonie Fantastique* and *Roman Carnival* overture include perfected versions of material previously used in his early *Messe solennelle*, so is Puccini's *Capriccio sinfonico* (1883) the source of the opening Bohemian motif in *La bohème*.

Although he would later settle at Torre del Lago, an idyllic lakeside village a few miles from Lucca, by the age of twenty Puccini knew that he needed to broaden his musical experience, and in order to do so would have to leave Lucca. The reputation of the conservatory in Milan was comparable to that of the Paris Conservatoire and the city's opera house, La Scala, was every young Italian composer's symbol of success. It was for La Scala that the boy Mozart had been invited to compose his mammoth opera, *Mitridate*, for La Scala that Rossini had written *Il turco in Italia* and *La gazza ladra*, for La Scala that the Sicilian-born Bellini's *Norma* and *Il pirata* were destined, and for which Verdi had composed his first four operas.

Positioned just south of the Alps, Milan was an international city, ruled for much of the nineteenth century by Austria. Wagner's music flourished there. Stendhal spent some of his best years there. Manzoni, in *I promessi sposi* ('The Betrothed'), chronicled its seventeenth-century sufferings under the Spaniards from a nineteenth-century

The Milan Conservatory, housed in a convent attached to the church of Santa Maria della Passione, was founded in 1807. It was here that, through his mother's determination, the twenty-two year old Puccini enrolled as a student.

standpoint. *I lombardi*, Verdi's fourth opera, proclaimed through its patriotic choruses the pursuit of Italian unification at a time (1843) when Milan was still under Austria's thumb and Italy as a whole remained crudely divided between that country and France. The infant Verdi, for a time, had been hidden for safety with his mother in a bell tower in the Duchy of Parma.

Later, with a wealth of lyric theatres at his disposal throughout the length of the Italian peninsula, Verdi – by then left-wing – was quick to recognize opera as a weapon of political propaganda and of patriotism, just as Wagner simultaneously did in Germany. By the middle of the nineteenth century opera had become a hugely popular art form, adored by Italian people of every class; it was not at all the supposedly 'élitist entertainment' condemned by today's tabloid press. And because of its popularity, it soon developed – in Milan and Rome, Naples and Palermo, Venice and Vicenza, Parma and Pesaro, and every small town proud enough to possess its own small opera

house – into a heavy industry, with new pieces, new singers, new conductors and new experiences in constant demand.

Verdi's patriotic choruses – 'Va, pensiero' from *Nabucco*, 'O Signore, dal tetto natio' from *I lombardi* – were sung in the streets, and the composer himself was widely established as a nationalist hero when the political slogan, 'Vittorio Emanuele, Re d'Italia' ('Victor Emmanuel, King of Italy'), was reduced to its emotive initials, VERDI. Milan became northern Italy's operatic powerhouse, a mecca for singers from all over Europe. When the Risorgimento, Italy's movement for political unification, successfully took flame, the Austrians were soon evicted from Lombardy and the French, thanks to Garibaldi, were driven from the south.

If Verdi had known that, over a century later, Italy would be progressing again towards disunity, with Umberto Bossi's Lega Nord loudly announcing Mantua to be the future capital of a new North Italy called 'Padania', he would have been shocked to discover the possible fate of his political ideals. Yet when he became a member of the original central parliament in Turin, he seldom bothered to take his seat in the house. Indeed he very soon resigned. Politics, for Verdi, took second place to music, and in the scheme of Puccini's priorities would come infinitely lower.

It was certainly not for political reasons that Puccini in 1880 was to journey northwards from Lucca to Milan through a recently united Italy. Music, underpinned by a desire to leave his hometown for a while, was the driving force that prompted him to try his luck as a student at what was generally considered to be the best conservatory in northern Italy. All he needed was funding. But as a fatherless lad without the means to study away from home, he could hardly be said to possess the best of prospects. It was then, however, that his mother's powerful Tuscan pertinacity paid off. She was aware that Alfredo Catalani, also from Lucca, was already studying in Milan. Four years Puccini's senior, he was the future composer of one of Arturo Toscanini's favourite operas, *La Wally*, but would turn out (through illness and various psychological problems) to lack Puccini's musical staying power.

In the hope that her son would receive the same benefits as the plainly inferior Catalani (whose *La Wally* has nevertheless recently gained international attention thanks to the popularity of one of its

Queen Margherita of Italy, who was successfully approached by Albina Puccini to come to the aid of 'a poor mother and an ambitious boy'. The royal scholarship Puccini received made possible his studies in Milan.

arias), Albina Puccini asked her rich unmarried Uncle Nicolao for help. Nicolao, happily, approved of his great-nephew and agreed to contribute towards the cost of three years at the Milan Conservatory. For the rest of the money, Albina was advised to contact Queen Margherita of Italy, who granted royal scholarships to gifted but impoverished music students. Claiming that her son was the youngest of a 'dynasty of musicians', she asked the queen to come to the aid of 'a poor mother and an ambitious boy'. The line could have come from a Puccini opera, but it did the trick.

Though the scholarship was by no means generous – one hundred Italian lire per month for a year, with the proviso that Uncle Nicolao pay the rest – it was sufficient to make Milan a feasibility (Albina herself lived on a mere sixty-seven lire per month, with which she had to support the fatherless family). Accordingly, Puccini applied to sit the Conservatory's entrance examination, which would entitle him to a year's probation. Verdi, before him, had famously failed the test. Puccini, reporting to his mother that the questions were 'ridiculously simple', not only passed but came top. Nine days before Christmas he installed himself in frugal lodgings where there were innumerable house-rules, including a ban on playing the piano at night. Against this unpromising background, his lessons began.

Amilcare Ponchielli, composer of *La gioconda*, and Antonio Bazzini, composer of a pre-Puccini version of *Turandot*, were his principal teachers. Tales of his wild and irreverent behaviour abound, many of them confirmed by his letters home. Even these, however, should perhaps be taken with a pinch of salt. Was Ponchielli really so absent-minded that – as Puccini reported to his mother – 'I bring him the same homework I prepared for Maestro Bazzini. I even submitted to him the same fugue three or four times over with only the slightest changes.' No doubt this was true, but Ponchielli was clearly nobody's fool. He, too, wrote to Puccini's mother, telling her that her son was one of the best pupils in his class, but adding: 'I should be extremely satisfied if he applied himself to his work with a little more assiduity, for, if he wants to, he can do it very well.' Puccini's contrapuntal exercises, preserved in various archives, bear out Ponchielli's words. As one Puccini scholar has remarked, they are 'conscientious student work', putting paid to the tales of the composer being lazy and offhand in his studies.

Opposite, Amilcare Ponchielli (1834–86), opera composer and tutor at the Milan Conservatory. He considered Puccini one of his best pupils, but wished that he would apply himself more assiduously.

Pietro Mascagni (1863–1945), the composer of *Cavalleria rusticana*, shared lodgings with Puccini in Milan. Some of their student pranks later found their way into Puccini's *La bohème*.

Yet it is plain that he was only partly absorbed in his classes in Milan. Composition lessons he enjoyed, on the whole, because he was good at them and moreover could see why they were important. And Ponchielli, whatever his qualities as a teacher, was a talented man. Compulsory lessons in dramatic literature and aesthetics, on the other hand, bored him rigid, even though they were relevant to his future career as an opera composer. His jottings on this course, which ultimately found their way back to Lucca, are filled with exasperated exclamations, among them: 'Ciao, professore, io dormo' ('Bye-bye, professor, I'm asleep').

But, miles away from his mother, he was learning how to survive, and to be resourceful. His brother became a fellow-lodger, and, more influentially, so did the nineteen-year-old Pietro Mascagni, who was to write *Cavalleria rusticana* a few years later. When creditors called at the lodgings, Puccini and Mascagni would take it in turns to hide in the wardrobe and say the other was out. Their suspicious landlord, however, proved more astute. When Puccini's monthly allowance arrived from the queen, the envelope would be slit open before he received it, and the rent extracted. But when he came to compose *La bohème* – where the landlord of the bohemians' garret is mercilessly portrayed as a buffoon – Puccini got his revenge.

In other respects, too, his experiences at that time must have stood him in good stead. When he needed cash to lavish on a young dancer from La Scala, he pawned his overcoat. A touching aria about the pawning of a favourite coat would later appear in *La bohème* (it was indeed forced into the opera, irrespective of its suitability). When Mascagni cooked lunch – an activity rigorously banned by their landlord – Puccini played the piano loudly in order to conceal the rattle of pots and pans. Puccini's student pranks are well recorded, and are in nice contrast to the severely sober photographs of the man in his maturity. Catalani, already heading towards an early death at the age of thirty-nine from tuberculosis, rarely joined in the fun, but Mascagni, before he and Puccini grew jealous of each other (and later their wives tempestuously joined in the fray), was an eager participant.

Academically, however, they had little in common. Puccini made up for his horseplay by actually working quite hard at his studies. Mascagni could not bear academic life, and soon ran off to join a travelling opera company. But although his career took fire quicker than Puccini's – *Cavalleria rusticana*, still one of the hits of the Italian repertoire, was proof of his early talent – he did not possess Puccini's self-discipline, and it soon showed.

Puccini himself, in his letters home, left a vivid description of how he spent his days in Milan. Rising at eight-thirty, he said, he would go to his lessons, if he had any; otherwise, in what seemed a fairly desultory way, he practised the piano in his bedsitter ('a rather pretty room ... clean and tidy ... with a polished walnut writing-table that is a real beauty'), stopped for breakfast at ten-thirty, then went out. At one o'clock he returned and worked for four hours. At five he went out again for a 'frugal' meal, consisting of three plates of soup, followed by 'some other things to fill up with', a piece of Gorgonzola cheese, and a half-litre of wine. Already a budding dandy, he would then light a cigar and saunter through Milan's magnificent Galleria Vittorio Emanuele, between La Scala and the Cathedral, perhaps stopping at a café en route. At nine, he returned to his lodgings, resumed work, then went to bed with a book. 'And that,' he told his mother, 'is how I live.' Doubtless it was an edited version of his activities. He already had an eye for the girls, and would entertain them in the Osteria Aida, a well-known hostelry, even if he was not

yet interested in a liaison of greater consequence such as that between
Rodolfo and Mimi in *La bohème*.

What spare cash he had went on café life and an occasional visit to
the opera to see Meyerbeer's *Étoile du Nord*, Auber's *Fra Diavolo*, or, if
he was lucky, Verdi's *Simon Boccanegra*. Though his arrival in Milan
failed to coincide with a major Verdi première – *Otello* was not
unveiled at La Scala until 1887 – it did coincide with the opera house's
installation of electric lighting in place of gas. But what he really
longed for, as he confided to his mother, was a can of Tuscan olive oil,
in which he could cook white beans. In this respect he remained a
true Lucchese, unseduced by Milanese fripperies.

But it was music that really mattered. With his finals looming at
the Conservatory, he began composing his *Capriccio Sinfonico*, which
preoccupied him wherever he went – 'in the street, in class, and at the
Osteria Aida'. He wrote on 'odd sheets, scraps of paper, and the
margins of newspapers'. The fifteen-minute piece, though progressive
enough in style to baffle Ponchielli, won him his diploma along with a

Puccini's diploma from the
Milan Conservatory was
awarded on the strength of
his orchestral *Capriccio
Sinfonico*. Although the music
had evidently baffled
Ponchielli, it was publicly
performed by the
Conservatory's student
orchestra under Franco
Faccio, future conductor of
Verdi's *Otello*.

public performance by the Conservatory's student orchestra under the conductorship of the talented Franco Faccio, whom Verdi would later choose for the première of *Otello*.

In a Milanese newspaper appropriately called *La Perseveranza*, the *Capriccio Sinfonico* was warmly acclaimed – not, admittedly, for any theatrical qualities it contained, but because of its 'specifically symphonic' ones. Since the critic, Filippo Filippi, was noted for championing both Verdi and Wagner, his review was taken seriously and Puccini, at the age of twenty-five, suddenly made his name. Symphonic or not, the *Capriccio Sinfonico* was an orchestral reservoire into which he was later prone to dip. Some of the music found its way into his second opera, *Edgar*, as well as into *La bohème*.

Doubtless considering the rest of the score to be expendable, if not embarrassing, Puccini later withdrew it from the Conservatory library and never returned it. He failed, however, to destroy it, and more than one recent recording has shown it to be a somewhat clumsy but otherwise thoroughly attractive piece of juvenilia. In spite of Filippo Filippi's comments, it often sounds quite operatic in quality, complete with a certain amount of posturing. There is also a delightfully buoyant and clearly recognizable use of the music that would eventually form the opening of *La bohème*. Far from seeming to be out of keeping with the orchestral *Capriccio*, the operatic element positively enhances it, not least when the orchestral equivalent of Marcello's voice is heard emerging from the orchestral texture. As with the *Preludio Sinfonico*, there is a prayer-like ending. The overall effect is that of a substantial concert overture and, if given the chance, it would surely enjoy some success among music-lovers who regret that Puccini's orchestral repertoire is so meagre.

Having established, in however small a way, a definite identity, Puccini now needed to flesh it out with music of greater consequence. Rather than return to Lucca, where he might easily have been sucked back into a world of church music or, worse, into teaching ('classrooms,' he once declared, 'give me claustrophobia'), he decided to stay in Milan. And Ponchielli, who believed in him, soon took up his cause.

First he introduced Puccini to Italy's leading music publisher, Giulio Ricordi, and then to a possible librettist, Ferdinando Fontana;

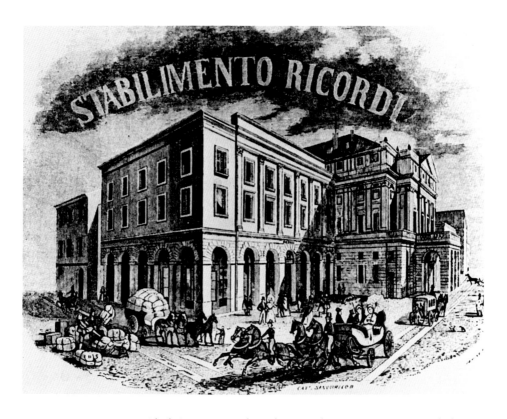

The original premises of the Casa Ricordi, Italy's leading music publishers, was next door to La Scala in Milan. With Verdi and Puccini as their leading composers Ricordi soon expanded around the world.

with their support and involvement the young composer might be given the incentive he needed to produce his first opera. These were astute moves, although it was the link with Ricordi which, in the long term, really mattered. Today, brash branches of the House of Ricordi sell compact discs, cassettes, video tapes, and all manner of electronic gear, but in Puccini's time they were famous for just one thing: the publication, within charming art nouveau (or what the Italians prefer to call 'Liberty style') covers, of the cream of Italian music, especially if it was operatic. Puccini, it soon became apparent, counted as cream. Ricordi, recognizing this, would later publish all but one of his operas.

Yet getting the right start was, as so often, a matter of luck as well as of genius. For Puccini, the luck lay in an invitation to a hotel, Il Barco, between Lecco and Bergamo, on the edge of the Italian Alps to the north of Milan. Il Barco belonged to Antonio Ghislanzoni, librettist of Verdi's *Aida*, and it was there that Ponchielli – again proving himself a shrewd and effective organizer – engineered a meeting between Puccini and the writer Fontana. The aim, as soon became apparent, was to try to talk Fontana (who was a journalist and therefore, it was feared, someone capable of pressing a hard bargain) into supplying Puccini with a libretto on the cheap.

There was a degree of urgency about the meeting. Puccini was eager to enter a competition, promoted by a Milanese tycoon called Edoardo Sonzogno, for the composition of a one-act opera, and he needed to find not only a librettist he could work with in a hurry, but also a subject. Sonzogno's musical interests were not entirely altruistic. His many business operations included a musical publishing firm – a rival to Ricordi's – and the ownership of a Milan theatre, the Teatrico Lirico. Needing fodder for both, along with maximum publicity, he arrived at his idea for a competition.

Yet it was not a competition like any other. One-act operas of the sort Sonzogno visualized were a new challenge to Italian composers. In the past, as had been demonstrated by Pergolesi, Rossini, and Donizetti, there had been one-act comedies, but Italy, like the rest of Europe, was approaching an age when operatic terseness, allied to dramatic subject matter, was to give opera a fresh intensity – and, it was hoped, a new reality – of utterance. Mascagni's *Cavalleria rusticana*, Leoncavallo's *I pagliacci*, Strauss's *Salome* and *Elektra*, Zemlinsky's *A Florentine Tragedy*, and Schoenberg's *Erwartung* would all be milestones of the genre; so would Puccini's *Il trittico* and, to a lesser extent, *Le villi*, which was the work he entered for Sonzogno's competition in 1883.

His deadline was tight. The *Capriccio Sinfonico* had had its first performance in July. The opera had to be completed by 31 December. Fontana seemed disappointingly intent on a good fee. 'I shall not write a libretto for less than three hundred lire per act,' he declared. But since Puccini wanted only a single act, and as Fontana decided in the end to reduce his fee to one hundred lire because he thought libretto writing might prove an 'appealing and amusing occupation', the project suddenly became possible. Moreover, and quite promisingly, Fontana considered that a 'strong current of sympathy' flowed between him and Puccini. He had heard and enjoyed the *Capriccio Sinfonico*, and proposed the macabre subject-matter of *Le villi* as suitable for a one-act opera. Puccini accepted, and by

September the libretto was written. Puccini, seldom the fastest of workers, had three months in which to produce his score.

Though he eventually became astute, and notoriously hard to please, in his choice of texts, Puccini at this point was still all too plainly a novice. The Gothic grotesquerie of *Le villi* might have suited Carl Maria von Weber, a composer who, in the famous phrase of the musicologist Donald Tovey, 'poured his talents into a pig trough'. But, with its Black Forest setting, its medieval background, its vengeful ghosts of maidens abandoned by their lovers, and its climactic dance of death, this operatic equivalent of Adolph Adam's popular ballet, *Giselle*, was utterly alien to the Puccini we have come to know. Why he accepted so fey a libretto is hard to say, but the likeliest answer lay in a vogue for the supernatural, and for the embracing of evil, that had crossed the Alps into Italy from southern Germany.

In Milan a group called the Scapigliatura, or 'Bohemians', of which Ponchielli and Ghislanzoni were both members, had been formed in the 1860s to rid the city of what was deemed (at least by them) to be Italian provincialism and to let in some literary, albeit decadent, fresh air. The name derived from Henri Murger's Parisian *Scènes de la vie de bohème*, which Puccini would eventually transform into a work that exultantly transcended its source material.

Meanwhile the poetry of Heinrich Heine, Germany's self-styled 'Last Romantic', was being cultivated by these young Italian aesthetes, who also soaked themselves in the works of Hoffmann and Baudelaire. Arrigo Boito, a leading member of the group, composed his *Mefistofele* a decade after Charles Gounod's charming but watery version of *Faust* in an attempt to give Goethe the opera he really deserved. As a gifted librettist, he also provided Ponchielli with the text for his operatic glorification of evil, *La gioconda*. Alfredo Catalani, one of the group's younger Wagner-fixated members, raked through German mythology for his subject matter, although his musical style remained unmistakably Italian.

As Ferdinando Fontana was also a member of the group, it was inevitable that he would try to lure Puccini into its twilight world. And, with his morbid ghost story, he succeeded. It was the first and last time that Puccini would accept a libretto without question and without considerable self-debate. But on this occasion he knew that he had no time to lose. Not only was he a slow worker, he was often

Puccini, right, with his first librettist, Ferdinando Fontana, who claimed that a 'strong bond of sympathy' flowed between them. Puccini, however, soon progressed to other and better librettists.

indecisive, and though capable of recycling material when he thought something was worth using twice, he never did so with the audacious gusto of a Rossini. To write *Le villi* he needed every available minute, his only interludes being the piano lessons he gave in order to raise enough money to live on. These, however, had one far-reaching outcome. Among his pupils was Elvira Gemignani, *née* Bonturi, the young wife of one of his Lucca schoolmates, with whom he was soon to elope.

The manuscript of *Le villi* was delivered on the very last day, and written with the untidiness for which this otherwise fastidious man

became notorious. His efforts proved in vain. *Le villi* was rejected as illegible, without anyone attempting to unravel it, although the real reason for its rejection may simply have been that it had arrived too late for serious consideration – there were, after all, twenty-seven other contenders. The prize of two thousand lire was divided between two nonentities, Guglielmo Zuelli and Luigi Borelli. Though their award-winning works were staged soon afterwards in Milan, neither composer today earns a mention in musical dictionaries.

The failure of *Le villi* was enough to make Puccini despair. Although he had already begun to reveal the pessimistic streak that was to grow in him from work to work, he responded on this occasion with what seems to have been remarkable composure. This was at least partly due to the influential Fontana, who was determined that his industry on the libretto would not go wasted. As a result, Puccini found himself invited to a supper party at the house of the wealthy Milanese, Marco Sala, where he was expected to sing excerpts from his opera. So affectingly did he do so that the guests contributed enough money to stage his piece (how fortunate composers would be if this were to happen today).

Nor was this all. The House of Ricordi agreed to print the libretto, and Boito persuaded a theatre manager to give the opera three performances. Puccini's career was on the move. Ricordi was one of the magic names in the world of Italian music, an old Milanese family firm founded in 1808 by Giovanni Ricordi, leader of one of Milan's theatre orchestras. At the time of *Le villi*, it was in the hands of Giovanni's shrewd pianist son Tito, who had developed more advanced printing methods, had gained the Italian rights of Wagner's operas, and immediately recognized Puccini's potential.

For a while its premises adjoined La Scala, but the Casa Ricordi was soon to spread throughout Italy. There were mergers with rival firms. Branch offices opened in other countries. Yet in spite of its increasing commercialism, it has remained a major publisher, with Verdi and Puccini as the continuing jewels in its crown, and with new editions of the works of Rossini and Donizetti as ongoing projects.

It was with Tito's son Giulio – the most gifted and musically perceptive of the Ricordis, hailed by Puccini as 'the best of poets, mender of other men's faults' – that the composer principally collaborated. Eighteen years older than his *wunderkind*, the benevolent but critical Giulio exerted a far-reaching and fatherly influence on the young Puccini's progress. Succeeding Tito in 1888, after the composition of *Le villi*, he oversaw the publication of *Edgar*, *Manon Lescaut*, *La bohème*, *Tosca*, *Madama Butterfly*, and *La fanciulla del West*, before he in turn was succeeded by his son, another (but considerably less tactful) Tito. By then forty-seven, the new Tito had worked as an engineer and was regarded by Puccini as a bull in a china shop. Mutual antagonism led to one of Puccini's last operas, *La rondine*, being published by a rival publisher. The rift, it is true, did heal, but almost too late. By the time Puccini had reached *Turandot*, the firm was no longer Ricordi property.

Amazingly, the success of *Le villi* – nurtured by the earlier Tito – proved greater than the first night of *Madama Butterfly* twenty years later. Three items were encored. The Teatro del Verme was packed. The critics were happy. As the influential *Corriere della Sera* remarked: 'We have here not a young student but a Bizet or a Massenet.' Scorn was vented on the stupidity of the competition jury that had 'tossed Puccini aside like a bit of rag'. The composer wired his mother (by then fatally ill in Lucca) that *Le villi* had had eighteen curtain calls.

Verdi, without actually seeing the piece, wrote a testimonial of sorts, saying that Puccini was 'well spoken of', though he should guard against 'symphonic tendencies' in his music. 'Opera is opera,' Verdi pontificated, 'and symphony is symphony, but inserting symphony into opera is not necessarily a good thing.'

Symphonic form, in fact, has never been a powerful Italian preoccupation. It was the German and Austrian composers, from Haydn onwards, who relentlessly developed the art of the symphony from a diminutive eighteenth-century orchestral format to works as vast, romantic, and elaborately structured as Beethoven's *Eroica*. Italy, on the other hand, devoted itself increasingly to opera after its enthusiasm for baroque instrumental tone – employed in concertos and sonatas inspired by Stradivari and the other great Italian instrument makers – had run its course. Solo instruments and solo voices, in a sense, proved interchangeable. Yet Verdi, in his appraisal of *Le villi*, had astutely placed his finger on what today may be perceived as a dichotomy in Puccini's score. Described in its publicity material as an 'opera-ballo', it was a compromise containing too little song and too much orchestral dance.

Recognizing its structural imbalance – or perhaps simply knowing that one-act operas can be difficult to market – Ricordi invited Puccini to rewrite his music in two acts, adding, as bait, a commission for a second opera, which would be performed at La Scala. Even the two-act version of *Le villi*, however, now seems imperfectly assembled, though its première in Turin on Boxing Day 1884 was as enthusiastically greeted as the one-act original. But thereafter its success began to falter.

At La Scala in January 1885 the music was thought to be orchestrally too heavy and 'Wagnerian'. At the San Carlo, Naples, a few months later it was booed. Yet to have his first opera launched in a succession of major Italian theatres showed that Puccini was at least being treated seriously. Fontana's libretto – about vengeful spirits who pursue a fickle young man for having caused the death of his beloved – may have been maladroit, but the music triumphed over it. To the story of the insensitive Roberto, forced to dance himself to death after his neglect has prompted his beloved Anna's suicide, Puccini succeeded in bringing a degree of the immediacy for which he would later be famed. The stilted Germanic background, and the inclusion of lines such as 'May your beauty be accursed, you vile whore', were obstacles he surmounted with impressive aplomb.

The ominous orchestral introduction can today be said to bear Puccini's recognizable stamp. The funeral march at the start of Act II, bluntly and unexpectedly denoting the death of Roberto's beloved, can be identified as one of Puccini's early masterstrokes – an intermezzo of a sort which Mascagni, who played in the pit at the first performance of *Le villi*, would later copy to advantage. The grinding tarantella that succeeds it is equally striking in the way it transfers an obsessive southern Italian dance to the depths of a German forest. The spoken narration, tightening up the action between the first and second acts, adds an extra ingredient to Puccini's operatic recipe, anticipating Stravinsky's *Oedipus Rex* by more than forty years. Yet it was a device he never used again (it might later have helped to solve some of the structural problems of *Turandot*).

Roberto's music, including one fine aria, is enticing enough to have induced at least one present-day international star tenor, Placido Domingo, to record it. The love duet with Anna, the opera's unhappy heroine, is no less eloquent, even if it lacks the melodic distinction of

Following page, the Teatro del Verme in Milan, less famous than La Scala but with a more tolerant audience, was the scene of the successful première of Le villi in 1884.

Puccini's later works. Anna herself is evidently the prototype of all Puccini's so-called 'little' women – although unlike Cio-Cio-San in *Madama Butterfly* (an opera of which *Le villi* contains some foretastes), she gets her revenge in the end. *Le villi* may not be a masterpiece, but as evidence of a tiro composer flexing his operatic muscles it is pretty good all the same. Indeed, its portents of genius make it still well worth championing, as sympathetic productions occasionally demonstrate.

2

Puccini in 1889, the year of
the première of *Edgar* at La
Scala, Milan

*Almighty God touched me with his little finger
and told me to write for the theatre – mind,
only the theatre.*

Giacomo Puccini,
vowing to follow in Verdi's footsteps

Breakthrough 1885-93

To call *Le villi* a false start would be to show a faulty grasp of the twenty-five-year-old Puccini's personality as an opera composer. Behind its improbable Gothic exterior the music is of sufficient quality to make it seem as promising a first opera as Verdi's sombre *Oberto* or Rossini's delicious *L'inganno felice*. What it lacks is obvious enough: the surefire melodies, the sharp-edged characterization, the subtly impressionistic orchestral colouring, the precisely calculated sense of pace we associate with the mature Puccini – all still lay in the future. But the fingerprints were undoubtedly there. All the music needs, if a case is to be made for it today, is sheer quality of performance. This does not necessarily mean casting someone as starry as Domingo in the role of the anti-hero, and it certainly does not mean opting for Pavarotti – at least if the final death dance is to have any credibility. But the voice and style of a Carreras might suit it admirably or, better still, a young discovery with enough panache to portray Roberto with real conviction. *Le villi* is a young man's opera. It demands a youthful performance and a conductor who genuinely believes in it.

Yet people who have never seen *Le villi* are content to say that Puccini did not 'find' himself until he reached *Manon Lescaut* – and even then not completely. The claim is true, but only up to a point. And it is undoubtedly unfair to the young Puccini, who was here trying out, as he was to do throughout his career, ideas that were not only interesting in themselves but would serve as springboards to his next opera. In fact, if he did not find his musical identity in *Le villi*, he was already some distance towards doing so. He went even further in *Edgar*, his second opera, which took him five years to complete. Even as a young man, Puccini never moved at Mozart's lightning speed, and he was already revealing a psychological inability to say of one of his works that he had completed it to his satisfaction.

But *Edgar* was worth the trouble it caused him. True, one should not state the case for it too highly. That would be almost as foolish as to make grand claims for *Le villi*. The surefire melodies are still not quite there. Yet, along with the assured orchestration we have grown to expect of the composer of *La bohème*, they are certainly getting closer. What really matters, however, is that *Edgar*, on its own terms, is a succulent operatic *fritto misto*, a real Italian fry-up of mixed ingredients spiced with touches of Bizet's *Carmen* and Wagner's *Tannhäuser*, of Ponchielli and Verdi, recognizable enough to be savoured by Italian audiences of the period. Today, its flashbacks to *Le villi* and, more fascinatingly, some curious touches of Berlioz – the Byronic and Faustian sides of whose musical personality it emulates – are similarly recognizable. Along with its anticipation of *Turandot* in the way it sets a gentle heroine against a ferocious one, it is a work that holds a distinctive position in the Puccini canon for anyone patient enough to accept its shortcomings.

Its problems lie principally with the crudity of its libretto and the absurdity of its subject matter. Libretto problems were to prove a running theme of Puccini's operatic career, although he would soon learn how to cope with them better. Meanwhile he was not yet fully ready, and was, moreover, carrying an artistic burden. Between the completion of *Le villi* in 1884 and that of *Edgar* in 1889, he was for contractual reasons stuck with the maladroit Ferdinando Fontana as his creative partner. The man who had initially seemed a promising librettist, and who considered himself Puccini's superior, was no longer the best of prospects.

Yet these were not wasted years. Puccini learnt a lot during them, about the art of opera and about life in general. His life, indeed, was proving quite eventful, in spite of his still meagre financial resources, and his every action in the 1880s was to have a bearing on his future.

They were years of change, and of private grief. Back home in Lucca, his beloved mother – the most central figure in his life until then – had died in 1884, and her death had cut him deeply. 'Whatever triumphs art may bring me,' he declared, 'the loss of my dear mother means that I shall never be really happy.' Yet to claim, as did his Viennese-born biographer Mosco Carner, that Puccini in his subsequent operas was imprisoned by 'a neurotic fixation which may be defined as an unresolved bondage to the mother-image' was perhaps being too Freudian. The composer later installed, in her memory, a new organ in the church of San Nicola, where one of his sisters was a nun. But in the meantime it was hardly coincidental that, as a typically Italian mother's boy, he found what seemed a suitable replacement for her in the person of Elvira Gemignani, even if one questions his long-term wisdom in doing so. Elvira Gemignani, first as his mistress and eventually as his wife, would torment him – and he her – throughout most of their life together in the same way as the errant Roberto and the vengeful Anna tormented each other in *Le villi.*

Elvira Gemignani, Puccini's pupil, his mistress, the mother of his son and ultimately his wife. Her fiery temperament may have initially been one of her attractions, but it contributed to the deterioration of their relationship.

When Puccini grew involved with Elvira, she was the wife of Narciso Gemignani, one of the composer's former schoolmates, an amateur baritone who worked as a wholesale liquor merchant in Lucca. Puccini is thought to have known her before her marriage, under her maiden name of Elvira Bonturi, but whether he was already attracted to her has never been confirmed. But it was Gemignani who married her, and who appears to have lived quite happily with her until he rashly encouraged her to go to the young composer for piano and singing lessons.

Elvira was soon Puccini's star pupil, at least in the sense that he was greatly attracted to her, and she to him. The fact that she had a husband and two children did not deter him from impulsively pursuing her, and, as is often the case in these situations, the desire to live dangerously doubtless increased their initial ardour. While his mother – who was hardly likely to have approved of such a relationship – was alive, he took good care to conceal the affair from her. When she died – and he, temporarily isolated in Milan, suddenly needed someone to play the role of mother as well as lover – Elvira demonstratively consoled him by moving north in 1886 with her six-year-old daughter, Fosca, the elder of her two children, and setting up house with her penniless teacher while her three-year-old son, Renato, remained at home.

Elvira was a handsome young woman, with what was described as a flashing Italian temperament – one way of saying that she was potentially a bit of a scold – and with a will as strong as that of Puccini's mother. Puccini himself was not always so strong-willed, though in terms of Tuscan good looks he was considered quite a catch. Even when short of money, he had an instinctive sense of *la bella figura*, the Italian art of good grooming. He coiffed his hair and trimmed his moustache. He wore smart Italian shoes. Though reputed to be tall, he looks rather stockily built in many of his published photographs – a fact rather confirmed by the statue of him (if it can be trusted) on the waterfront at Torre del Lago. But he was certainly dapper. Within two years he and Elvira had a child of their own, Antonio, who was destined to remain illegitimate until the death of Elvira's husband eighteen years later made it possible for the boy to become a Puccini.

Lucca was not a town to take Giacomo's or Elvira's misbehaviour lightly, and they were never forgiven by the friends and family of

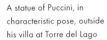

A statue of Puccini, in characteristic pose, outside his villa at Torre del Lago

Elvira's abandoned spouse. Their life together, therefore, built as it was on scandalous foundations, proved turbulent. As in many other unhappy relationships, the qualities that first attracted them to each other were among the ones they subsequently came to hate. Puccini's sisters, who disapproved of the liaison from the start, did their best to cause trouble. But Elvira's sister Ida was even more hostile. Rightly knowing Elvira to be a possessive and jealous woman, she sought to undermine her trust in Puccini by telling her he was fickle. The amount of damage she caused is easy to guess. Whether or not Puccini was unfaithful to Elvira in these early years is not known, but he certainly became so later.

Yet in his own way he stood by her. His various other relationships, whatever heart-break they caused Elvira, were for the most part trivial and short-lived, frequently no more than one-night stands. Apart from Elvira herself, there was no long-term love in his life (although at least one of his loves developed into a long-term friendship of a closeness he never experienced with Elvira herself) and there was no question that he would ever run off permanently with someone else. There were ways in which, as a strong if often house-bound wife, she had him quite firmly under control.

The women he seemed really to love – and it is a fascinating psychological point – were the heroines of his operas: the more he distanced himself emotionally from Elvira, the more he loved his heroines. In both *Le villi* and *Edgar*, he concerned himself with the fate of a man torn between contrasted women. The faithful Fidelia and tigerish Tigrana in *Edgar* are Puccini's equivalent of Bizet's Micaëla and Carmen, and, indeed, of Elvira and whatever other woman might be in Puccini's life. Edgar himself – a by no means uninteresting personality to find in an immature opera – not only combines Byron with Berlioz, but Tannhäuser with Faust. Loved by Fidelia, but enticed away from her by Tigrana, he escapes from both of them into the army. The scene where Edgar, disguised as a monk, witnesses his own funeral – he is assumed to have died in battle – would have appealed to Berlioz, composer of *Harold in Italy*. Edgar, upon revealing his true identity, is briefly reunited with Fidelia, whom the vengeful Tigrana stabs to death while Edgar collapses in tears as the curtain falls.

But if Fidelia and Tigrana appealed to conflicting aspects of Puccini's personality, Manon Lescaut, as he admitted, was the first of

his characters he really adored. She was, he declared, 'a heroine I
believe in and therefore one who cannot fail to win the hearts of the
public'. Yet even while he was believing in her he had already cast his
eye on the prospect of Tosca, a heroine he had longed for but had
been prevented from possessing in 1889 (when he saw Sarah Bernhardt
play her in Sardou's drama) because she was not yet legally available
for operatic treatment. Even as a composer, then, Puccini was
potentially promiscuous. Had he been able to get his hands on Tosca
in 1889, he might not have turned to Manon. Yet, as we shall see, he
devoted himself to Manon, and before he could be sure that he had
got her right he turned loose no fewer than five librettists on her
(seven if we include the composer's own contributions and those of
the publisher Ricordi).

Five librettists might have made a difference to *Edgar*, especially if
they were the ones Puccini finally chose for *Manon Lescaut*. Not that
poor Fontana yet seemed to be the wrong man. Indeed there is a
stylistic consistency between *Le villi* and *Edgar* that Puccini could
have continued to exploit if he had felt like it. In many ways the one
work is a fascinating revamp of the other. Each has Gothic overtones,
a similar setting, a tug between morality and immorality, and a funeral
cortège. Edgar's Byronic personality is noticeably akin to Roberto's in
Le villi, and Fidelia is a more human Anna. But in performance, in
spite of its fascinating idiosyncracies, *Edgar* seemed turgid and its
libretto inept. Although Puccini was aware of its imperfections – he
was aware of imperfections in all his operas, and constantly sought to
rectify them – he might have been tempted at this point in his career
to write another work in the same vein, in the hope of getting it right
at the third attempt.

Instead, after one of his typical delays, he wrote *Manon Lescaut*,
which was a different sort of opera altogether. Posterity has blessed
him for it, yet it seems a pity, all the same, that he never produced his
perfect *Edgar*. But even the imperfect *Edgar* is a work worth hearing.
Its source – a five-act verse drama by Alfred de Musset entitled *La
Coupe et les Lèvres* ('The Cup and the Lips') – would admittedly have
tested the patience of Job. Yet what Puccini (and, let it be said,
Fontana) made of it is by no means deplorable. In its own peculiar
way it hangs together. Andrew Porter, in an essay in *The New Yorker*,
has called it an 'arresting' piece – 'an abrupt, violent, existentialist, and

curiously modern drama – formal and symbolic, not veristic'. Nothing in it, he added, is explained; actions are shown, not motivated. In another article he went further, declaring it to be the only one of Puccini's operas that could confidently be recommended to Peter Brook or Peter Hall to work upon as director. As for Wieland Wagner, he could have 'done wonders with it'.

Why, then, did *Edgar* fail, not only at its Scala première – a fate understandable enough, in spite of the excellent cast and conductor who were recruited – but more or less ever since? Even Puccini himself, during that first performance on Easter Sunday 1889, got cold feet about it, and later confessed that he had always thought it an unsuitable subject for an opera. Admitting the result to be more his fault than Fontana's, he said: 'It was an organism defective from the dramatic point of view.'

But that was wisdom after the event. The Scala audience was, in fact, quite uncharacteristically considerate. Surprisingly in the circumstances, nobody booed. Puccini himself was applauded, but rightly sensed polite defeat. His *succès d'estime* was not enough to sustain more than three performances, especially as the critics, while admiring the singers, were generally unimpressed by the piece. One reviewer went so far as to call *Edgar* a 'sin against art'. Others voiced their disenchantment more tactfully, and a few were genuinely encouraging. Giulio Ricordi, who had pinned his faith in Puccini and had paid him three hundred lire a month while he wrestled with – as the composer put it – a 'work of such importance and difficulty', nevertheless found himself having to explain to his shareholders that things had gone wrong.

Giulio Ricordi, admirable publisher that he was, did not lose faith in his protégé, whom he had proclaimed to be the 'crown prince' among Italy's possible successors to Verdi. The shareholders, on the other hand, insisted that Puccini was an expensive failure who should be dropped forthwith. The Verdi comparison, however well intentioned, was admittedly unfortunate, and in the long run it did Puccini considerable damage. He was not a composer in the heroic Verdi mould. He was a different sort of composer altogether, and even today his music is made to suffer unnecessarily through a comparison that was, from the beginning, quite irrelevant – except in the sense that he was Verdi's only successor of any stature.

Following page, La Scala and its piazza in Milan. The opera house's façade was not ostentatious, but the interior, as Puccini discovered, could become a scene of deep personal humiliation if the audience showed contempt for one of his works.

To ease Puccini's depression, Ricordi sponsored him in a visit to
Bayreuth that summer for a performance of Wagner's *Die
Meistersinger*, a work for which the firm had recently acquired the
Italian rights. Exposure to Wagner, Ricordi felt, could only be
beneficial. More pertinently, he declared a degree of belief in *Edgar* by
saying that Fontana had at least supplied Puccini with two effective
acts, even if the rest of the text contained 'much obscurity'. The
composer, he said, had done the best he could in the circumstances.

The question was whether the work was worth revising for a
further series of performances. Elvira, who had belittled Puccini's
efforts from the start by reminding him that Verdi had composed
Rigoletto, *Il trovatore*, and *La traviata* in the same space of time, was
beginning to show what sort of companion she really was. There was
no doubt that Puccini's domestic circumstances were already proving a
hindrance rather than an inspiration to his work. Some composers –
Haydn and Mozart most obviously – could rise above domestic
difficulties. In Puccini's case they made a slow worker even slower.

Yet out of the mood of melancholy that followed *Edgar*'s
unpromising baptism there grew in Puccini a desire to rescue the
piece. Even before the première, Puccini had simply wanted to run
away and hide. He had written to his brother Michele, by then in
South America, to find out if there was any employment available over
there – 'not,' as he put it self-laceratingly, 'in Buenos Aires, but in the
interior among the redskins.'

What eventually dissuaded him – apart from Michele himself, who
was as impoverished in Argentina as he had been in Milan, whose life
was clearly wretched, and who was soon to die of yellow fever – was
the opportunity to restructure *Edgar* with the help of judicious cutting
(something he would later have to do also to *Madama Butterfly* after
its much less savoury Scala reception) and with the hope of a revival
the following year. The proposed revival fell through, causing more
chagrin, but a successful production in Lucca's charming little Teatro
Giglio provided compensation on a local-boy-makes-good level.

A subsequent production in Madrid carried more weight, especially
as Francesco Tamagno, who had created the title role in Verdi's *Otello*,
was persuaded to sing Edgar. Puccini had wanted him in the first place
for Milan, but in Madrid, alas, he turned out not to be the alchemist
who would transform *Edgar* from a failure to a success, even in its

'The only person who
inspires me with trust and to
whom I can confide all that
is going through my mind':
Puccini's comment on his
trusted publisher Giulio
Ricordi, who claimed his
protégé to be the 'crown
prince' among Italy's
possible successors to Verdi

The cover of the revised three-act version of *Edgar*. This version won applause in Puccini's native Lucca but flopped elsewhere. The composer, a lover of puns, inscribed his copy of the score with the words 'E Dio ti Gu A Rdi da quest'opera' ('May God preserve you from this opera').

abbreviated form. The work failed again, as it also did in a third and even more abbreviated version, in Buenos Aires. In the end, Puccini – who enjoyed puns – inscribed a score of *Edgar* with the words, 'E Dio ti Gu A Rdi da quest'opera' ('May God preserve you from this opera').

Puccini preserved himself from it through hard labour on *Manon Lescaut,* though isolated performances around the world have tantalisingly breathed hints of life into it. People in recent years have been learning to tolerate the crudities of an opera composer's early works – Verdi, in particular, springs to mind – for the sake of getting at the good music they often contain. One of the continuing obstacles to *Edgar's* success has been the low opinion of it purveyed by some of Puccini's most ardent literary champions. William Ashbrook, for instance, could find nothing more enthusiastic to write of it than that it is 'filled with conscientious, if rarely inspired, craftsmanship'. The great Puccini biographer, Mosco Carner, echoed the composer himself by calling it quite simply a 'blunder', and Charles Osborne complained vaguely of its failure to 'show character in action'.

Sometimes a composer's established champions can also be his worst enemies. There is no point in reading David Brown's generally magnificent four-volume biography of Tchaikovsky in order to find out why, for example, you adore the Second Piano Concerto, because all Brown tells you is that it is a rotten work. There is no point in listening to more than the first three movements of Schubert's great C major String Quintet if your adviser happens to be Arthur Hutchings, who calls the finale 'café' music. Deryck Cooke's authoritative dismissal of the vast opening movement of Mahler's Third Symphony as 'a total formal failure' may likewise seem perfectly persuasive until you actually listen to, and find yourself caring about, the music he has dismissed.

Without claiming *Edgar* to be a work of the calibre of Mahler's Third Symphony, I would nevertheless call it a case in point, for it is an opera that has been maligned for perfectly correct but irrelevant reasons. As blunders go, it is less of a blunder than Richard Strauss's *Guntram*, though less of a masterpiece than Benjamin Britten's *Peter Grimes* – to mention two operas by composers who, when they wrote these works, were of roughly the same age as Puccini when he wrote *Edgar*. It contains, as even its detractors generally agree, music too good to lose. At Puccini's funeral service in Milan Cathedral in 1924, it was not for nothing that Toscanini insisted on conducting the requiem section of *Edgar* (although this perhaps revealed wishful thinking on Toscanini's part, since it portrayed a character who was not actually dead). Far from being mere craftsmanship, this was music – as Toscanini well knew – that would stir the souls of all who heard it.

But to listen – in the absence of an opportunity to see the work more than once, with luck, in a lifetime – to Lorin Maazel's recording is to become convinced that there is more to *Edgar* than the requiem music, and that even the libretto is not beyond hope. The plot comes to seem more consequential when you observe how Puccini actually handled it. Although Bizet, Gounod, Wagner and Berlioz all contribute to Edgar's personality, the voice is unmistakably Puccini's. The women in Edgar's life may seem mere type-casting, but Puccini gives them vibrancy.

Edgar, in fact, is a type of psychodrama, which suggests, from the distance of its fourteenth-century disguise, what it is like to be present at your own funeral, or how it feels if, for no strong reason, you decide to burn down your own house. Viewed from these angles, it is a Puccini opera as irresistible as any other, and one that shows the young composer dealing with operatic ingredients he would never encounter again – a genuinely romantic hero, a drama of the mind, an anti-realistic story unfashionably tackled at a time when other Italian composers were turning to the art of crude naturalism, or what became known as *verismo*.

If Puccini had followed *Edgar*'s path further, where might he have gone? The question is academic, but the curious poetic power of the piece is enough to justify its being asked. If *Edgar* had not failed at La Scala – and if it had earned Puccini the seven thousand lire he was counting on – the remainder of his career might have progressed quite differently. Andrew Porter, not stopping at his previous praise, has hailed it as 'perhaps the most striking of all Puccini's operas', which is a bit like saying that *Zaïde*, because of the novelty value it possessed at the time it was written, is the most striking of Mozart's operas. Yet in the sense that each shows its composer trying out ideas (in Mozart's case the use of spoken words accompanied by music) that, for one reason or another, he would henceforward shun, the claim is perhaps justified. *Edgar*, whatever the composer himself chose in the end to say about it, was not really a blunder at all.

Nor, more obviously, was *Manon Lescaut*, the work with which, for most people, Puccini's career began. It cost him, if anything, even more trouble to write. Domestically, at any rate, his life had for the moment improved. No longer able to afford living in Milan – not least because his previously benevolent Uncle Nicolao, by now virtuously disapproving of Elvira, had demanded his money back – he had been on the lookout for somewhere more permanent to stay.

Temporary lodgings here and there had made the young couple constantly aware that they were living in sin, and there had been a particularly embarrassing moment when one of their landladies, on discovering that they were not married, curtly flung them out.

On hearing that a gamekeeper's house could be rented at Torre del Lago, between the seaside resort of Viareggio and his native Lucca, Puccini jumped at what would provide him with the opportunity to

Puccini the huntsman: the local palmipeds [webbed-footed birds], he reported, panted for his 'murderous and infallible lead', but the accuracy of his aim remains open to question. To gain advantage, however, the wily composer ensured that he was given exclusive rights over all other huntsmen on Lake Massaciuccoli.

compose in peace, go shooting, and avoid the glare of puritanical eyes. Shooting was already his favoured pastime. 'After the piano,' he famously declared, 'my favourite instrument is the rifle.' And though elsewhere it was considered a rich man's sport, in Italy it was indulged in by one and all – as it still is today. New laws, brought into being around 1990, are said to have made the mass obliteration of birds more difficult, but Italians traditionally find ways around such problems.

Though he did not yet know it, Puccini had found what would be his home environment for most of his career. Torre del Lago would become associated with him in the same way, if not to the same extent, as the Bavarian town of Bayreuth is associated with Wagner or Aldeburgh in Suffolk with Benjamin Britten. Although not a native of the village, he imposed himself firmly upon it, living first in one and then in another abode. Moreover, unlike Wagner at Bayreuth, he could argue that at least he was a native of the area.

But whereas Wagner lived a conspicuously public life, building his own theatre, to his own radical design, for the performance of his (and only his) works at what remains to this day a place of annual ritualistic pilgrimage, Puccini lived at Torre del Lago simply for the sake of its privacy. Not only did he want to escape the scandal that surrounded his life with Elvira, he also needed absolute peace in which to compose. Although his operas were shorter and less ambitious than Wagner's – in the sense that he did not aim to make each of them a Wagnerian *Gesamtkunstwerk*, or 'total work of art', in which music, drama, poetry and design would be unified as a single art-form – they cost him at least as much trouble to write. *Le villi* may have been produced at speed, but he was never to work as fast again, and he was already aware, thanks to his experience with *Edgar*, just how slow and indecisive a composer he was.

So Torre del Lago was the perfect place for him. It was quiet. It was blissfully beautiful and yet had a severity that would prevent it from becoming vulgarly commercialized. When he felt like company, he could pop into Lucca to see old friends. Even today things are not so very different from how they were in Puccini's time – a few more houses, a shop or two, the Butterfly Restaurant and the simple open-air Puccini theatre on the lakeside are about all that have been added, while the Puccini villa itself has become his shrine, just as Wahnfried is a shrine to Wagner.

But the much photographed Puccini villa, now a museum, was not his original abode at Torre del Lago. The gamekeeper's house he first rented was a more modest and temporary residence. Before acquiring somewhere permanent, he needed to discover whether Torre del Lago suited him, and whether people would respect his privacy there. The composing of *Manon Lescaut*, which cost him another three years of his life, would be the test. By 1895, when it received its first performance at the Teatro Regio, Turin, he knew he had come to stay.

To what extent the villagers welcomed the presence of an increasingly famous, but still scandalous, composer was another matter. With village bluntness, they disapproved of his operas and described them as 'harlot's music'. They knew enough about his private life to disapprove of that, too. And though once established he brought a degree of employment to the place – his villa needed a staff – this would tragically backfire on him some years later when one of his servants killed herself after Elvira wrongly accused her of having an affair with her husband. Life at Torre del Lago by that time, as people gloatingly remarked, had become a bit like one of Puccini's own operas.

The waterfront at Torre del Lago, with Puccini's villa. Quiet and secluded, yet within easy reach of the composer's native Lucca, the village suited the private side of his personality to perfection. It was here that he most often went shooting, and here that he composed most of his operas.

But that was a while off yet. The Spanish production of *Edgar*, which began his journey to fame outside Italy, marked the start of what was to become an established Puccini practice. Wherever one of his works received a major (or even sometimes a minor) production abroad, he himself went along in an advisory or supervisory capacity. Since the age of the 'creative' producer, armed with a 'concept' different from that of the composer and librettist, had not yet dawned, Puccini's task was not too strenuous. He needed to be no more than a watchdog, ensuring that the staging, and the performance, were up to scratch. Had he possessed conducting ability, he would doubtless have played a more active role in his own music. But since he had no such experience (unlike Wagner or Britten), he

Puccini pictured with Arturo Toscanini (right). Their relationship was uneasy and sometimes hostile, but Toscanini was an important supporter and interpreter of Puccini's operas, starting with the première of La bohème, which he conducted in 1896.

always had to leave that task to others, reserving for himself the right to express his own strong and influential opinions on who should conduct what.

In this respect he was lucky, quite early in his career, to win the support of the fiery young Arturo Toscanini. Their relationship, though seldom equable, sometimes explosive, and at least once almost irredeemably antagonistic, was firmly established with the première of *La bohème*, which Toscanini conducted in 1896, and it endured right to the end of Puccini's life, when the unfinished *Turandot* was closely guarded by the great conductor until he publicly unveiled it, in the composer's memory, at La Scala in 1926.

The passion with which Toscanini treated Puccini's music was clearly to the composer's taste. Even as a twenty-two-year-old novice, conducting it for the first time, he had galvanized a revival of *Le villi* at Brescia's Teatro Grande in 1890, thereby bringing himself to the attention of the thirty-one-year-old composer. What Puccini described as the conductor's 'poetry' and *'souplesse'* – not qualities other people found in the often brusque, hard-driven Toscanini approach to music – increasingly won the composer's admiration. Even though Puccini came to agree with Toscanini's dangerous suggestion that parts of *Manon Lescaut* needed reorchestration, he could nevertheless turn with lightning Italian speed against the conductor if he felt that he had been slighted by him in some way. Far from being in Puccini's words a 'great soul', Toscanini then immediately became 'wicked', 'treacherous', 'heartless' and 'full of envy'.

Gustav Mahler (1860–1911); the Austrian composer conducted *Le villi* in Hamburg, but he held Puccini's most famous operas in low esteem and refused to conduct them in Vienna.

Yet Toscanini was just one, though admittedly the most distinguished one, of an impressive tally of conductors upon whom, at a time when conductors mattered infinitely more than producers, Puccini proved able to draw from the very start of his career. Even Gustav Mahler did his youthful bit for Puccini by conducting *Le villi* – whose spooky teutonic elements he must have appreciated – in Hamburg during his own prentice years. But when Puccini's subject-matter grew less Gothic and (in Mahler's view) more commonplace, he withdrew his approval, refused to conduct Puccini's works at the Vienna Opera, and (to the Italian composer's chagrin) laughed mockingly during the Viennese première of *La bohème*.

Puccini's travels abroad, as well as around Italy, formed the obverse of his periods of withdrawal at Torre del Lago. He enjoyed big cities, even if he never wholly cared for Milan. They gave him the freedom from Elvira he increasingly needed, and they enabled him to indulge in the discreet little sexual adventures which evidently mattered so much to him. As a quietly flamboyant Italian, he needed to prove his manhood, and the older he grew the more vital this became. But before *Edgar* gave him his first opportunity to visit Spain – it was his first major trip abroad – Giulio Ricordi took pains to warn him that 'the climate of Madrid is treacherous, especially at night ... not to mention other things!!!!'

Ricordi's advice was soon to prove helpful in artistic matters, too. Recognizing Fontana to be a write-off as a librettist, he proposed a replacement who was destined to have a far-reaching effect on Puccini's career. His name was Giuseppe Giacosa who, along with fellow-librettist Luigi Illica, would form with Puccini a triumvirate of peerless quality. The three of them would be responsible for the librettos for *La bohème, Tosca* and *Madama Butterfly*. Meanwhile *Manon Lescaut* was to be their testing ground.

They were, in fact, more than a triumvirate. With Giulio Ricordi as an essential component – urging, advising, discussing, admonishing and inspiring – they were very much a quartet. Just because he was only indirectly involved in the creation of Puccini's operas did not make Ricordi any the less important. Their round-the-table dialogues, principally in Milan, would have been fascinating to eavesdrop upon. Cynical people have likened them to business meetings, and have sought to demean Puccini's genius because of it. Yet they gave him just the working framework that his inspiration required. In this respect, Ricordi was more than a publisher. Himself a lapsed opera composer, he understood Puccini better than anyone else. What an outstandingly good editor is to a novelist, Ricordi very definitely became to Puccini.

And from the beginning, Puccini definitely needed him. His career took wing, but his self-confidence did not. He remained full of uncertainties of a kind from which one could never have imagined the supremely self-confident Wagner or Liszt suffering. Even the choice of subject for an opera cost him dearly. Although he finally produced a dozen works, he seriously contemplated about seventy others. He fluttered from one notion to another, enthusing then rejecting, never making up his mind.

When he had finally decided upon a subject, and had settled down to writing, a whole new range of problems would be unleashed. The libretto had to be just right, and its piecemeal arrival on his desk had to keep pace with his inspiration. Demands for changes and more changes would be made to an increasingly sullen Giacosa or Illica. A proposed three-act structure would be reduced to two acts then increased again to three. The balance of *Madama Butterfly*, and ultimately of *Turandot*, caused him endless trouble. But each one of his operas did so in one way or another.

Yet this was the way his inspiration worked, and at least the finished product repaid the effort. He may have been a less ambitious and visionary opera composer than Modest Musorgsky, who sought painfully to portray the splendours and miseries of Russian history in operatic terms, but he did not leave his works in a shambolically unfinished state. And to the charge that he did not set his aims as high as Verdi's, that he lacked Verdi's 'idealism' and 'spirituality', one would answer that his standards were very high indeed – even if his idealism

The great triumvirate: Puccini (left) poses with his two long-suffering librettists, Giuseppe Giacosa (centre) and Luigi Illica (right). With Giulio Ricordi as their adviser, they produced *La bohème*, *Tosca* and *Madama Butterfly*.

and spirituality were of a different sort. No, he was not a Verdi, and he had no need to be. He was a child of his time, the most significant member of the post-Verdi generation, and there was no doubt that he towered over his Italian rivals, such as Catalani and Mascagni, in the same way that Verdi had towered over his own contemporaries.

To hail him as Verdi's heir, as Ricordi so determinedly did, may nevertheless seem misleading. If anything, he was Verdi's antithesis, in the sense that the profound humanism of Verdi's music was replaced in Puccini's by the decadence of a period that was also to produce Richard Strauss's *Salome*. Where Verdi addressed himself to large-scale heroic subjects, Puccini tackled smaller, more domestic ones, substituting tenderness and sometimes sadism for Verdi's grandeur of sentiment. Yet Verdi's heir he undoubtedly was. There was, after all, nobody else who could have been.

Giacosa and Illica, in combination, were to become Puccini's greatest librettists, but they were not his first choice for *Manon Lescaut*. Having finally discarded Fontana – who would momentarily reappear in his life many years later with a proposal to adapt Oscar Wilde's *A Florentine Tragedy* as an opera – Puccini wanted to choose his own subject rather than have one foisted upon him. And from then on his subjects would be foolproof ones, scrupulously considered beforehand from all possible angles.

Topical plays and books, of already proven success, were what attracted him (as they also attracted Verdi). They gave him the sense of security he needed, though for some composers – indeed for many – they would have been a recipe for disaster. ('Opera as a Sung Play' is a phrase often employed by music critics with a note of contempt.) Although Verdi succeeded with *Otello* in 1887, Debussy with *Pelléas et Mélisande* in 1904, and Berg with *Wozzeck* in 1927, these were exceptions that proved the rule. Good plays are complete in themselves and transforming them into operas can, in general, only enfeeble them. But the point about Puccini is that he did not choose good plays. He chose popular, even trashy, plays or stories, and transcended them in the same way as Schubert transcended the words of many embarrassing poems by turning them into marvellous songs. Sardou's *Tosca*, even if enacted by today's equivalent of Sarah Bernhardt, would probably be unwatchable. Puccini's *Tosca*, however sensational its subject matter, is a masterpiece.

Yet in deciding to tackle the Abbé Prévost's novel, *Manon Lescaut*, Puccini took a considerable risk, in that it had already been successfully set by Jules Massenet. In one sense, this was taking the philosophy of playing for safety to extremes: the fact that Massenet had made an opera out of *Manon Lescaut* proved that it was a good subject for an opera. But Massenet, sixteen years older than Puccini, was an already established composer and his *Manon* was a very popular opera, not only in France but beyond. In blatantly setting out to rival it, the Italian novice was playing with fire. The story of a weak young nobleman's fatal passion for a fickle young *demi-mondaine* was something very different to the subjects of his two previous works –

Jules Massenet (1842–1912), the French composer whose *Manon*, according to Puccini, was all 'powder and minuets'

that must have been part of the attraction – but there was no obvious reason to suppose that he would know how to capture the refinements of a classical French novel. What he did know was how to personalize his relationship with its female protagonist. As he confidently put it: 'Manon is a heroine I trust and therefore she cannot fail to win the hearts of the public. Why should there not be two operas about her? An inconstant girl such as Manon can have more than one lover.'

In 1952 a third composer, Hans Werner Henze, would woo the Abbé Prévost's promiscuous heroine in a successfully updated treatment of the story which he entitled *Boulevard Solitude*. Puccini's instincts had been again proved sound. Though self-confidence of this sort was unusual in him, he did possess a competitive streak and, for the time being, a degree of youthful recklessness. Explaining, at least by implication, why he thought himself better equipped to deal with the subject than Massenet, he declared: 'Massenet feels it as a Frenchman, with the powder and the minuets. I shall feel it as an Italian, with desperate passion.'

Puccini felt it with the minuets, too, as it happened. Around the time of writing *Manon Lescaut* he had been dabbling in the art of the string quartet, not to the extent that he proved capable of producing a work as complete as Verdi's solitary masterpiece in the form, but enough to produce a handful of isolated movements. Among these were three charmingly melodious minuets, delicate pastiches of the style of his great Lucchese predecessor, Luigi Boccherini. Although concert programmes today rarely feature the minuets, there exist recordings of them which can be heard with pleasure as tiny chips from the Puccini workshop.

Such pieces were an exercise he would find useful when he wanted to convey the gracious background atmosphere of parts of *Manon Lescaut* (where the first of Puccini's own minuets is actually quoted during the dancing lesson in Act II) and one other of his quartet movements proved even more helpful. This was the piece he had entitled *Crisantemi* ('Crysanthemums'), a touching and haunting minor-key elegy on the death, in January 1890, of the triple-titled Prince Amedeo of Savoy, Duke of Aosta and King of Spain. Puccini later said he composed it in one night, but it sounds better and more carefully worked than that. The Campanari Quartet's initial performances of it in Milan and Brescia were a success, and today this melancholy *morceau* continues to carry a quiet emotional charge far beyond its apparent slightness of scale. The composer himself, when the time came, valued it highly enough to incorporate its two exquisite principal themes in Act III of *Manon Lescaut.*

Meanwhile there was still the more important question of a libretto to consider. Puccini had made it plain that he did not want another Fontana, but Giacoso and Illica were not yet installed as his collaborators. The preliminary choice was Ruggero Leoncavallo, better known as the composer of *I pagliacci,* but at this point in his career still showing tendencies towards the written word – especially the writing of librettos. The astute Giulio Ricordi had had his eye on him for some time, and commissioned him to prepare a draft for Puccini to consider. The trouble was that Puccini, himself more astute than he used to be, did not like it. Next in line was Puccini's young friend, Marco Praga, who was less experienced than Leoncavallo but seemed likely to be able to comply more precisely with the composer's wishes. Being purely a prose writer, Praga set to work in partnership with the poet, Domenico Oliva, and the finished product was read aloud to Puccini at Giulio Ricordi's summer house on Lake Como.

In spite of the lure of Lucca and its surroundings, a great deal of the background work on Puccini's early operas took place further north, in the peaceful atmosphere of villages near the deepest and most scenic of Italy's great lakes. It was partly a matter of expedience. Most of his important contacts lived in or around Milan. *Edgar* had been completed at Caprino Bergamasco, in the hills between Lecco and Bergamo, because that was where Fontana spent much of his time and Ghislanzoni ran his artists' hotel, Il Barco. Today the tiny village is dominated by a restaurant and stables called La Staffa ('The Stirrup') and nobody seems to remember Il Barco.

In the winter of 1890, in order to ponder at leisure the libretto for *Manon Lescaut,* Puccini rented a chalet not far from Ricordi's expensive lakeside residence at Cernobbio, site of the Villa d'Este. Leoncavallo, by then at work on *Pagliacci,* was staying nearby, and the two composers teased each other by hanging competitive posters from their windows. Leoncavallo's appropriately represented a clown (*un pagliaccio*) – his opera was to be staged in Milan (though not at La Scala) in 1892. Puccini's, more subtly, was a hand (this being one of his puns, *mano* meaning hand in Italian).

In the winter of 1890, while struggling with the composition of *Manon Lescaut*, Puccini rented a chalet near Giulio Ricordi's residence at Cernobbio, site of the Villa d'Este on Lake Como. The work was completed by 1892 thanks to the bracing air and the presence of Ricordi – 'that mender of other men's faults'.

But, struggle with it though he did, the libretto by Praga and Oliva failed to inspire him. It was then that Ricordi – that 'mender of other men's faults' – played his trump card and brought Giacoso and Illica into the picture. The Piacenza-born Illica, though moody and touchy, was an experienced librettist – Giordano's *Andrea Chénier* and Catalani's *La Wally* were among his other achievements. And although he was prone to defend his honour by fighting duels, in one of which he had lost part of an ear, he proved not impossible for Puccini to cope with. By the autumn of 1892, *Manon Lescaut* was finished. It had occupied three years of his life, and had involved as many as five librettists (along with literary contributions from the publisher and the composer himself), but for the moment, at least, Puccini was satisfied with it.

To avoid a possible repetition of the fate of *Edgar* at La Scala but also because Verdi's last opera, *Falstaff*, was about to have its première there, Ricordi arranged for *Manon Lescaut* to be staged at the Teatro Regio, Turin, with Alessandro Pomè, a veteran routinier, as conductor. There were uncertainties about the quality of the cast – Puccini, attending the rehearsals, expressed his fears that the singers would be inaudible – but the piece was an instant success. The thirty-year-old Cesira Ferrari, said to have been more of a singing actress than a potentially great soprano, portrayed Manon. Three years later she would create the role of Mimì in *La bohème*, and would be chosen by Toscanini in 1908 to be Italy's first Mélisande in Debussy's opera. Puccini was reputed to have been briefly in love with her, and she to have been briefly in love with Toscanini.

Although the rest of the *Manon* cast proved no more than adequate, the audience was elated enough to demand thirty curtain calls. The composer himself, at a huge celebratory supper, could do no more than murmur his blushing thanks, quite forgetting that he had prudently scribbled a speech on one of his cuffs.

Even the critics, who had gathered in Turin from all over Italy, gave *Manon Lescaut* their approval. It was noted that Puccini had decisively withdrawn from Wagner's mystic profundity, though in fact, as now seems perfectly obvious, the music at times steers uncommonly close to *Tristan und Isolde* in its use of voluptuous Wagnerian harmonies. Moreover the work has its own touching Wagnerian *Liebestod* in the

The handsome Teatro Regio, Turin, where *Manon Lescaut* and later *La bohème* had their first performances. It was in the same theatre that a special centenary production of *La bohème* was staged in 1996.

scene of Manon's prolonged 'love-death' in Act IV. Only Manon dies in this closing scene, whereas Isolde sings her *Liebestod* over Tristan's dead body. But Puccini's tenor hero (unlike Massenet's) is as good as dead at the end of *Manon Lescaut*, making the Wagnerian parallel more obvious. But Wagnerian or otherwise, Puccini had become a composer to reckon with, capable of creating, in the personality of Manon, a genuinely touching love-object. *Manon Lescaut* was very far from being a commonplace operatic melodrama.

When the opera reached Covent Garden the following year, Bernard Shaw (who perceptively detected a strong 'symphonic element' about the structure of Act I) declared that Puccini looked more like Verdi's heir than any of his rivals. Gustav Mahler, who had not yet decided to despise Puccini, conducted it with fervour in Germany. Money, for the first time in the composer's life, flowed in. Debts were paid off. Important academic posts in Milan and Venice were offered, but turned down. More important to Puccini was the

The Ricordi jacket of *Manon Lescaut*, Puccini's first real success. Cesira Ferrari, later to sing Mimi in *La bohème*, sang the title role. Puccini's profits enabled him to buy back the family home in Lucca, which had been sold after his mother's death.

chance to buy back the family home in Lucca, which had changed hands after his mother's death.

Yet *Manon Lescaut*, for all its virtues, was not yet the perfect Puccini opera. It is clearly a transitional work, albeit a remarkable one. The style in which it begins is not quite the style in which it ends. But the story, a sort of *Éducation Sentimentale*, suited Puccini very well. Manon, a teenage *femme fatale*, was someone with whom he found it easy to identify. The Chevalier des Grieux, her naïve and sentimental lover who destroys his life and career because of her, proved similarly sympathetic to him. With Massenet as his example, Puccini knew that the best way to treat the Abbé Prévost's short novel was as a series of lyric scenes, some of them roughly the same as Massenet's, others – to avoid accusations of plagiarism – deliberately different. But the biggest difference lay in the ending. Whereas Massenet compressed the climax of the story so that it closed with Manon's death on the road to Le Havre, Puccini pursued it to the bitter end in the desert outside New Orleans, where she dies in her wretched lover's arms after she has been deported.

To name one of these works as greater than the other would be ridiculous, but Puccini's in the circumstances was the greater achievement. He was a less experienced composer, and he did not have the Abbé Prévost's literary style at his fingertips in the way that Massenet had. The gear changes between one act of *Manon Lescaut* and the next lack naturalness, and the last act, after a powerful intermezzo in Puccini's most eloquent vein, loses a degree of momentum. But in our own time, more than one company has boldly attempted to get round the problem by presenting each act in a visually different style, sight and sound thereby complementing rather than contradicting each other.

With Act I treated as a conventional costume drama and Act IV as a Wagnerian abstraction, the passage of time can be compellingly underlined, even if the effect may seem somewhat mannered, indeed something of a concept. Concealing the work's stylistic contradictions is probably, in the long run, better than drawing attention to them. Puccini himself, born long before conceptual opera grew fashionable, would have deemed such a production to be enigmatically irrelevant. Musical performances of a high standard, with well-chosen singers and crystal clear stagings, were what he demanded and expected of an opera company. The strongpoint of *Manon Lescaut* lies in the wealth of fine detail with which Manon and the other characters are portrayed – the numerous, precisely observed touches that would become a Puccini speciality, separating him from more ordinary composers of his period. To obscure deliberately these features of his operas would have seemed to him a perverse act of sabotage.

Yet along with the finesse, there is also in *Manon Lescaut* a new spaciousness of musical design, underpinned by the almost symphonic structure that Shaw recognized in Act I, that gives the work real shape. Even the last act – in which Puccini self-indulgently prolongs the

Nelly Miricioiu as the money-loving Manon, with Raimund Herincx as Geronte di Ravoir, the Treasurer General, in Scottish Opera's production of *Manon Lescaut* at the 1982 Edinburgh Festival; Sir Alexander Gibson conducted.

promiscuous Manon's death after her deportation – sounds genuinely
expressive and moving when it is in the hands of a gifted soprano and
a perceptive conductor. Like the last act of Debussy's *Pelléas et
Mélisande*, the music is difficult to pace effectively. But just because it
is difficult does not mean it is impossible. In sparing his performers
and his audience nothing, Puccini was braver than Massenet, who
shirked the Louisiana denouement in his version of the story. And he
was brave, too, to restore Manon's central aria, 'Sola, perduta,
abbandonata' ('Alone, lost, abandoned'), which in one of his moments
of self-doubt he had decided to cut. It took Toscanini to convince him
of its emotional necessity, on the occasion of a thirtieth anniversary
performance at La Scala. Decisions never came easily to Puccini, and
from then on they would become even harder.

3

*After the piano, my favourite instrument
is the rifle.*

Giacomo Puccini,
on the pleasures of Torre del Lago

This caricature of Puccini by
Enrico Caruso suggests that
the two must have been close
friends. But Puccini's feelings
about the Neapolitan tenor,
whom he described as 'lazy
and too pleased with himself',
were always ambivalent.

The Years of Gold 1893–1904

In one of his books of memoirs, *Where I Fell to Earth*, the opera and literary critic, Peter Conrad, has written of how he became obsessed with the voice of his next door neighbour, a woman he regularly heard but never saw. As many as twenty or thirty times a day, she struggled through the opening phrases of the same operatic aria, then cracked on its first high note. He pondered upon the unremitting penance she subjected herself to, and nicknamed her Sisyphus the Soprano.

The aria she so valiantly and eternally tackled was 'In quelle trine morbide' from Act II of Puccini's *Manon Lescaut*, a nostalgic comparison between the life of luxury the heroine enjoys with her latest admirer and the humble apartment she previously shared with her beloved Chevalier des Grieux. Manon may have been no more than a *poule de luxe*, but the music is filled with what one can only call a genuine Puccinian passion and anguish. If *Manon Lescaut* marked the turning point in his career as an opera composer, then Manon's Act II aria was the turning point within that turning point. Like all Puccini's great arias, it is remarkably brief. Just when you are longing for more, it comes to an end. But then, succinctness was always one of the secrets of his success. He knew just how much of a good thing – or how little – to give his audience. And though his detractors have accused him of thereby manipulating his listeners, it was simply a gifted opera composer's instinctive ability to judge the timing of his music. In this respect, Puccini was quite phenomenally gifted, and 'In quelle trine morbide' was the first of a multiplicity of arias – ending with 'Nessun dorma' from *Turandot* – in which he put this particular gift memorably into practice.

Equally important, it was also his first aria capable of sticking instantly in the memory, in spite of an unpredictable design. Puccini's opponents despise him for that attribute, too, in the manner of Bach loftily inviting one of his sons to the opera by saying to him: 'Well, Friedemann, shall we go to Dresden and hear the pretty tunes?' In composing 'In quelle trine morbide', Puccini employed a bipartite structure of a sort he was to use many times again. For that reason, not everyone considers Puccini's arias to be spontaneous. Some people have cynically, and ridiculously, claimed that they were deliberately geared to fit one side of an old-fashioned shellac gramophone record, and even Mosco Carner, his most complete biographer, complained that 'In quelle trine morbide' was perfunctory and lacking in glow. But the qualities – in this case brevity and instant memorability – for which Puccini's arias have often been criticized are ones for which his devotees rightly adore him.

For all the virtues of *Manon Lescaut*, moments of such magical compression are still relatively rare. As the opera proceeds, a sort of Wagnerian breadth and harmonic richness undeniably tend to sweep aside the fine detail that is such an attractive feature of the first two acts. As Peter Conrad (in a different book) has put it, Puccini's Manon is a man-eating Isolde, and the score becomes invaded by the languishing disease of the *'Tristan* chord' – the innovatory and

Puccini with his son Tonio, who did not legitimately become a Puccini until the marriage of his parents in 1904

hauntingly yearning first chord of Wagner's opera of 1859, which cries
out for resolution and which pervades not only the whole of *Tristan
und Isolde* but, indeed, much of the future of Western music.

When, immediately afterwards, he began composing *La bohème*,
his vibrant picture of impoverished student life and love in the streets
and tenements of nineteenth-century Paris, Puccini made no such
mistake. Though the *Tristan* chord also appears in that work – most
noticeably when the consumptive Mimi first encounters her future
lover Rodolfo, in Act I – Puccini holds the Wagnerian invasion in
check. Here his ability to produce, and keep on producing,
distinctive melodies nearly bursts the work at the seams (in 1895
Puccini promised his publisher that it would contain 'as much
melody as possible'). Wagnerian longueurs are conspicuously absent.
Indeed *La bohème* is a work so racy that it must be one of the few
operas ever written that lasts not so very much longer in performance
than in a spoken reading of its libretto. What can make it seem long
is its four-act structure, prompting opera companies very often to eke
it out – in what can seem a spirit of sabotage – with no fewer than
three intervals. This may be good for a theatre's catering department
(who, for the sake of bar sales, would insert an interval in *Das
Rheingold* if given the chance) but it is not so good for Puccini. To
demonstrate what the removal of intervals can do for *La bohème*, the
Deutsche Oper, Berlin, once staged it in a single act, with the help of
a revolve, thereby giving a very different impression of the work's
running time.

But before writing *La bohème*, Puccini had to get *Manon Lescaut*
out of his system. More so than even *Le villi* or *Edgar*, this was the
work that embodied his Germanic leanings. Wagner's shadow looms
over the pages of its last act in a way that would never happen again to
the same extent in a Puccini opera. So perhaps it was after *Manon
Lescaut*, rather than before or during it, that Puccini really reached his
turning point. The gusto, the perfection of detail, the instinctive grasp
of timing, and the utter assurance of *La bohème* are enough to make
Manon Lescaut, for all its qualities, seem in comparison somewhat stiff
and heavy. Had he not written *Bohème* immediately afterwards, or had
he written it more Germanically, the straight comparison would not
arise, and we might even admire *Lescaut* for its lightness of touch.
Or perhaps not. Much of it, after all, is manifestly, and deliberately,

The Café Momus scene from the Deutsche Oper production of *La bohème*

weightier than the Frenchness of Massenet's *Manon*, and for that reason the light touches in the first half of the opera stand out all the more prominently.

Yet there is no doubt that between *Manon Lescaut* and *La bohème*, genius struck Puccini in the same way that it had struck Mozart between the eighteenth-century ordinariness of his second violin concerto, in D major, and the sudden unmistakable inspiration of his third, in G. In each case, something happened. How it happened is impossible to say. But when the moment arrived, Puccini knew how to seize it.

It is true that in his private life, there appeared to be a new state of well-being. The curse of Milan, except for business meetings, was largely behind him. The success of *Manon Lescaut* had given him the necessary reassurance that opera was his *métier*. Giacosa and Illica,

The final act of *La bohème*
in the 1963 production at
the Berlin Opera House

supported by Giulio Ricordi's vigilance and know-how, were librettists
he could work with. Domestically, things were in some ways more
settled. Not only did he have Torre del Lago to inspire him, he at last
had sufficient cash.

But there was an added stimulus, of a sort to which Puccini, with
his huntsman instincts, invariably reacted. In choosing *Manon Lescaut*
for a subject, he had believed he could do it better than Massenet – in
other words, he could outgun the Frenchman. With *La bohème* it was
the same, except that this time his opponent was a fellow Italian, his
old acquaintance and exact contemporary, Ruggero Leoncavallo.
Their friendship, such as it was, never recovered from their race to
transform Henry Murger's Parisian sketches, *Scènes de la vie de
bohème*, into an opera.

Though the more delicate details are unlikely ever to be known,
the course of their frequently misreported rift is largely as follows.
Within a month of the successful launching of *Manon Lescaut* in 1893,
Puccini let it be known that his next opera was likely to be *La bohème*.
As was to become habitual, however, he had other irons in the fire.
One of them, with Buddha as its improbable subject, never burned
very hot. But Giovanni Verga's *La Lupa* ('The She-Wolf') was
promising enough to prompt Puccini to visit the Sicilian author on
his home ground in grim Catania (birthplace of Bellini), thus causing
a dangerous postponement of *La bohème*. A Puccini opera based on
Verga's short story and stage play would indeed have been possible to
visualize, and the fact that it would have enabled him to out-Mascagni
Mascagni (whose melodramatic *Cavalleria rusticana*, composed in
1890, had a Verga story as its source) could have made it all the more
attractive to him.

But in the end, it seems, he found the characters uninspiring –
'without a single luminous or appealing figure to stand out' – which
presumably meant that he was unable to empathize with the earthy
peasant heroine (D. H. Lawrence, who settled for a while in the
nearby resort of Taormina and translated many of Verga's stories into
English, doubtless found her more to his taste). Nor did Puccini seem
much enamoured with Sicily itself, although the chance to respond to
its atmosphere, as well as to Verga, had been one of his reasons for
going there with some of his friends. Instead, at the first opportunity,
he headed for Malta, where the British authorities, failing to identify

him as Italy's most celebrated young composer, caught him taking snapshots of the British fleet and arrested him as a spy.

As a superstitious Italian, Puccini knew an ill-omen when he encountered one. During his voyage home from his meeting with Verga, he encountered another. Spotting the Contessa Gravina, Cosima Wagner's daughter (by her original marriage to Hans von Bülow), in the ship's cocktail bar, he deliberately attracted her attention by nonchalantly playing a selection from *Tannhäuser* on the piano. Then, engaging her in conversation, he told her that his next opera was likely to be about a passionate Sicilian woman who was murdered during a Good Friday procession. The Contessa, expressing shock, told the composer that such a revolting subject was not for him. Back in the security of Torre del Lago, Puccini duly reported to Giulio Ricordi that he was 'assailed by a thousand doubts' about *La Lupa*. The project was dead.

But by the time Puccini finally settled for *La bohème*, Leoncavallo claimed to be at work on the same opera. An acrimonious feud broke

Ruggero Leoncavallo, with whom Puccini had an acrimonious feud over who should compose *La bohème*. As Puccini succinctly put it: 'Let him compose, and I shall compose, and the public will judge.'

out between the two composers, first in a Milanese café they both
frequented, then in the Italian press – Puccini being supported by the
independent *Corriere della Sera*, Leoncavallo by *Il Secollo*, owned by
his publisher Sonzogno. Puccini, self-confident enough to know that
he held a winning hand, publicly and magnanimously declared: 'Let
him compose, and I shall compose, and the public will judge.'

By completing his opera before Leoncavallo, and by getting it
staged at the Teatro Regio, Turin, with the young Arturo Toscanini as
conductor, Puccini easily won the first round. Leoncavallo, on the
other hand, won the second. His *Bohème*, performed in Venice a year
later, proved more popular with the critics and public, and was
deemed – quite accurately, though not necessarily relevantly – to be
more truthful to Murger's text. Puccini, however, won in the end. His
was the *Bohème* which, once it gathered momentum, stayed the
course. Whereas Leoncavallo's more precisely characterized, and by no
means uninteresting, opera is today merely a collector's item, Puccini's
has gone from strength to strength as a staple of the international
repertoire, as alive in 1996 (when Turin's Teatro Regio, in common
with other opera houses, mounted a centenary production) as a
hundred years earlier.

Its distortion of the Murger original – in which Rodolfo, far from
being the romantic poet of Puccini's opera, was described as bald and
charmless, with holes in his sleeves and a 'huge, bushy, many-coloured
beard' – proved of no great consequence. In opera, as Joseph Kerman
has perceptively declared, the composer is the dramatist, and Puccini
extracted from Murger's novel the material he needed for what, after
all, would become a masterpiece far more famous than the book.

That he altered the personalities of the characters is undeniable.
But then, Murger – in drawing them from real life, and transforming
several of them into composites – had altered them also. What Puccini
did to Murger's *Bohème*, indeed, could be compared with
Tchaikovsky's well-intentioned (though uncomprehending) distortion
of Pushkin's *Eugene Onegin*. Puccini empathized with the frail young
Mimi – heroine of the opera but much less so of the book – in much
the same way as Tchaikovsky empathized with the gentle young
Tatyana, ignoring the irony and sarcasm of the written text in order to
convey his feelings for the person who appealed most to him.
Tchaikovsky, though homosexual, could imagine the plight in which

Tatyana found herself at the hands of the self-centred Onegin, and his responsiveness to her predicament was real enough. His ability to identify with the scorned Tatyana was powerful. Puccini, being heterosexual, could be said to have had the advantage in dealing with the sexual relationship of *Bohème*, yet it is hard not to believe that the character through whom he himself lived and breathed in this opera was the doomed Mimi, not the vain and feckless Rodolfo. Making her moonlit entry in Act I, she was the luminous and vulnerable figure he had been unable to find in Verga's *La Lupa.*

Puccini's ability to identify with his heroines, of course, was a major feature – perhaps *the* major feature – of all his operas. The fact that almost all of them were hard done by, and made to suffer for their charm, has prompted many commentators to claim that there must have been a sadistic element in his make-up, which he exploited musically. Some, indeed, have gone so far as to say that that was why he enjoyed shooting wild-fowl. But in fact it is impossible not to believe that he was on the woman's side every time, and that man's inhumanity to woman – or, in the case of two of his later operas, *Suor Angelica* and *Turandot*, woman's inhumanity to woman – concerned him deeply.

It also, in *La bohème*, inspired him to produce the most perfectly structured of all his operas, the one in which choice of subject, choice of librettists, and musical approach all merged to create a masterpiece. The problems he habitually faced in writing an opera were more satisfactorily resolved here than in any other work. His insatiable desire to tinker with what he had already written, stemming from his obsessive hope that he could always improve on it, was for once kept relatively under control. There was no need to tinker with *La bohème* after it had established itself – although inevitably, he desired to do so. But even he must have realized that, for once in his life, he had got things as right as he would ever get them.

The five librettists of *Manon Lescaut* had been reduced to the two who mattered, Giuseppe Giacosa and Luigi Illica. To say that Puccini trusted them would be to exaggerate. To say that, despite fierce disagreements, he knew he could work with them would be nearer the truth. Although their relationship seemed always on the point of collapse, it endured through this and two more major operas, *Tosca* and *Madama Butterfly*. These were the works by which Puccini's name

would become the most widely known, revered and accepted. As *Rigoletto, Il trovatore*, and *La traviata* did with Verdi, so they formed the halfway mark in his career. After them, he would strike out in different directions, and reveal a new sense of adventure for which he has not always been given full credit. Nevertheless *La bohème, Tosca*, and *Madama Butterfly* are the works for which the public continue above all to love him.

Opposite, a caricature of Puccini with his two librettists, Illica and Giacosa

Yet for all their apparent spontaneity, their composition as usual cost Puccini immense trouble. Although his librettists were given clearly delineated tasks – Illica was to write the scenario and Giacosa to versify it – both had to contend with the composer's volatile ideas on the work as a whole. Illica, envisaging an opera in five scenes, was soon complaining that he felt 'used, cast aside, taken up again, and once more shoved away like a dog'. Giacosa, protesting that one scene had had to be rewritten a hundred times, threatened to resign. Ricordi, appeasing Giacosa, provoked Puccini's impatience. 'All I wanted,' grumbled the composer, 'was that the work should be what it ought to be: logical, terse, and well balanced.' Illica, he added, should calm down and get on with the job.

By insisting on constant changes to his librettos, Puccini was already winning a reputation as a composer difficult to deal with. Compared with many of his predecessors, he also seemed inordinately slow. Yet he was by no means invariably so. True, *La bohème* took him three years, compared with the three weeks a Mozart might have needed for it. But when he was fully satisfied with the words, and inspiration was upon him, he could compose at speed. He could do so, moreover, with people around him. He was undisturbed by the sound of conversation in the room, his only stipulation being that nobody should hum or sing while he was at work, because that was something that not only distracted him but made him angry.

But if the actual act of composition was not always quite the problem it was reputed to be, the fastidious pre-planning and the ultimate dissatisfaction took up time. There was always something – a section of libretto that had not arrived or needed to be changed – that delayed his setting pen to paper. And in the end, when everything was done, there was his long-lasting belief that there might be another way, that a three-act opera could be reduced to two or increased to four, that the structure was somehow wrong, that the tone or

character of a scene had not been properly caught, that it was too
hard-edged or, alternatively, too soft.

Puccini procrastinated over these things to the extent that it is a
wonder how he ever permitted a new work to reach the opera house at
all. And he cared about them long after he released one in order to
move forward to the next. That was one of the reasons behind his
desire to attend – and, if possible, advise upon – every new
production of each of his operas, no matter how far afield he would
have to travel. No doubt it was also an excuse to escape from the
claustrophobia of domesticity, and to enjoy the odd amorous
adventure. But in our own time, perhaps only Benjamin Britten has so
possessively watched over the welfare of his works.

Yet unlike Britten – a composer whose sense of theatre, lyrical style
and penchant (especially in *Peter Grimes, Billy Budd* and *The Turn of
the Screw*) for sado-masochistic subject matter have made him seem
Puccini's operatic successor – Puccini showed no desire to exercise
strict control over his works by conducting them himself. This was a
field in which he had no expertise, although he was prepared to battle
with conductors over how his music should be performed. If a
conductor happened to be as strong-willed as Toscanini, the result
could be a major rift that took time to heal. But his troubles with his
librettists were what really preoccupied him, and they were relentlessly
pursued. The fiery Illica called them 'real battles in which there and
then entire acts were torn to pieces, scene after scene sacrificed, ideas
abjured that only a moment ago had seemed bright and beautiful;
thus was destroyed in a minute the work of long and painful months.'

Giacosa's reactions to what he regarded as Puccini's constant
interference were similarly truculent. About *La bohème* he complained
to Ricordi that he was sick to death of 'this constant re-making, re-
touching, adding, correcting, piecing together, extending on the one
hand and reducing on the other' that Puccini demanded of him. On
this 'trifling and uninteresting' duty, he grumbled, he was wasting up
to five hours a day, when he could more lucratively have been writing
articles. *Bohème*, he threatened, would be his last libretto, though in
fact he was to work with Puccini twice more, on *Tosca* and *Madama
Butterfly*, before he died in 1906 at the age of fifty-nine.

Considering that people generally associate an opera with its
composer rather than its librettist, it is easy to understand Giacosa's

disgruntlement. All that effort, he must have thought, for nothing! How ironic that he was destined to achieve lasting international success only through Puccini's reflected glory. He was, after all, a distinguished playwright and poet in his own right, just as Illica was an established and very professional (though less important) playwright and librettist.

Yet between them, beneath Puccini's lash, they helped to produce an opera built, as posterity has decreed, like a battleship. The four young men and two women, around whom the plot revolves, seem the very stuff of nineteenth-century bohemian life. Rodolfo and Mimi fall in and out of love, as do Marcello and Musetta, while Colline and Schaunard, without amorous entanglements, are content to assist in this little comedy of life. In the end Mimi dies. The others grieve. But Rodolfo, who finally is too self-absorbed to notice the actual moment of Mimi's death, will soon find someone else – or so his noisily ostentatious despair seems to imply as the curtain falls. The four men– poet, painter, philosopher, musician – are deftly differentiated. Mimi's sweetness finds its opposite in Musetta's brashness. Each scene, whether private or public, is a Parisian tableau precisely evoked by Puccini's music and by the conspicuous development, in this work, of his ability to express dramatic emotion in terms of memorable melody, and to respond instantaneously to every change of mood or situation. As one commentator put it: 'When he composed, he knew what he wanted; there was in him an inexorable cine-chronometer that followed all the action down to the smallest detail.'

Today, admittedly, that would be an accomplishment expected of any capable composer of film music. But *La bohème* was not film music and Puccini was not that sort of composer. In *Bohème* the music *is* the action, and the action the music, in a manner new to opera. That is what makes the vividly exact musical depiction of every incident in Act II unique in operatic history. Here is music in which time is not frozen in the manner it usually has to be in opera. Even the orchestral part, like the singing, is made to sound conversational in a fresh way, without sacrificing beauty of either instrumental or vocal tone. Nobody – except Puccini himself at one point in Act III of *Manon Lescaut* – had done anything quite like it before in Italian opera, and nobody would do it so successfully again.

Puccini in his study at Torre del Lago, with his Förster upright piano in the background. He worked amid a clutter of scores and manuscript paper, beneath pictures of Franz Lehár, Gustav Mahler, Enrico Caruso, Maria Jeritza and others.

Not for nothing did Mosco Carner hail *La bohème* as the first opera to 'achieve an almost perfect fusion of romantic and realistic elements with impressionistic features'. But for all its perfection of balance, Illica, in particular, seems to have been galled by Puccini's decision to jettison an entire act of the libretto, set in the courtyard of Musetta's house. Yet the composer's reason for doing so was dramatically sound. The action – in which bailiffs remove Musetta's furniture while she is throwing a party – would have been too similar to the hubbub of the preceding 'Café Momus' scene. The story would have begun to sprawl. But the fact that Leoncavallo made use of this episode, when he came to compose his own *Bohème*, must have irritated Illica even more.

In his constant desire to compress the subject matter of *La bohème*, Puccini was surely right. One of the work's special virtues is the way it enables lyricism to flower in an amazingly tight-knit setting. Act II – at the Café Momus – lasts a mere twenty minutes and benefits greatly from its concision. Never again, except in *Il trittico*, would Puccini produce music quite so mercurial or quite so perfectly calculated. And in the end, in spite of their complaints, Illica and Giacosa came to share his views on *La bohème*, even though they considered that he had distorted Murger's original. 'It's not,' as Illica succinctly put it, *'La bohème.'*

Illica was right. It was not. But for the world at large it ousted Murger's book and play. Puccini's lyricism, his blend of high spirits and sentiment, and his shunning of complex characterization were guaranteed to make the public identify with Mimi, Rodolfo, Musetta and Marcello and their various problems, even if Leoncavallo's earthier version got closer to the truth. If Puccini had never written his *Bohème*, would Leoncavallo's have been a success? Up to a point, perhaps, but for many people Puccini's *Bohème* remains the opera of operas.

Good productions of it – because the work itself is so perfectly tuned to a certain period and style – are able to endure for decades. Riccardo Salvadori's realistic décor for the original Turin production would be as viable today as a hundred years ago. Britain's now defunct Carl Rosa company toured its utilitarian old production from town to town for year after year, often in stirring performances, with no 'director' named in the programme. Covent Garden's original *fin-de-*

An early poster for *La bohème*, paying tribute to the original author as well as to Puccini and the two librettists. Puccini was accused of distorting Murger's original book and play in a way that Leoncavallo's opera did not, but there is no doubt that Puccini's was the more inspired version.

siècle staging was still in use, perfectly serviceably, a lifetime after it first opened, providing a vivid reminder of how Puccini himself liked his opera to look. Zeffirelli's tableau-esque production for La Scala, with Herbert von Karajan as its original conductor, likewise ran and ran, winning admiration for its exquisitely misty, Courbet-like décor and meticulous detail – the Café Momus and its surroundings were thronged with several hundred carefully choreographed people, and Puccini's stage band sounded like that of the Prussian Army.

Yet the work has not become mummified. When Baz Luhrman (best known for his film *Strictly Ballroom*) updated it to the 1950s for the Sydney Opera House, the results may have seemed no more than an Australianized version of a Hollywood hit – Fred Astaire and Audrey Hepburn in *Funny Face* were brought irresistibly to mind – but they possessed an exhilarating *élan*, even if the fine detail of Puccini's Act III, with its haunting evocation of the outskirts of Paris in the first half of the nineteenth century, were sacrificed in the process.

But no matter whether within its original picture frames or within modern ones, *La bohème* provides a richly rewarding portrait gallery upon which the performers can shed continually changing light. The visual acid test of a production's sensitivity to Puccini lies in whether Rodolfo's candle in Act I blows out accidentally, as it should do, or whether he blows it out himself in a crudely calculated attempt to seduce Mimi the moment he meets her. The latter approach – favoured, sadly, by Luciano Pavarotti, as well as by many other tenors and their directors today – to an opera that handles moonlight with poetic delicacy can only be called an ill-omen for the rest of the performance. Rodolfo, at this point in the story, must not seem as lacking in genuine tenderness as he does later. But musically, at least, the spuriously bawled-out ending to Act I, with the tenor striving towards a top C instead of gliding gently downwards to an authentic E, does seem to be a thing of the past, certainly in reputable opera houses.

Although Puccini has been criticized for turning Murger's *Bohème* into the tale of the poet and the seamstress, he did so with such flair, and with such a subtle interweaving of Rodolfo and Mimi with the other characters (especially Marcello and Musetta) that the opera works perfectly on its own terms. The student background is an affectionately remembered picture of Puccini's own student days in Milan – which must have been why, when he began to write Act I, his mind went back to his *Capriccio Sinfonico* and he made use of material from that student work for his rollicking opening scene. Never again would he persuade his librettists to give him a structure so beautifully balanced in his favour, so that Act I (high spirits followed by lyrical love scene) found its exact counterpart in Act IV (high spirits followed by tragedy). Likewise, the poetic detail of Act III showed it to be the lyrical obverse of the high spirits of Act II.

Nowhere else did Puccini give one of his operas such a recognizably and consistently symphonic shape. Leonard Bernstein had good reason to select Act III of *La bohème* as his favourite example of 'what music does to expand mere drama into opera'. Using it as the basis of a television lecture, he showed how successfully Puccini expanded the emotion of the words, how the change of one single note in a repeated phrase could heighten the drama, and how two, three or four characters singing simultaneously could create a network of emotions that was in itself a new kind of emotional experience – and one of a sort that only great opera can achieve.

When Puccini completed *La bohème* in his study at Torre del Lago at midnight on 10 December 1895, three years after he had begun it, he burst into tears, so great was his own emotion. Sentimental though it may seem, it was the death of Mimi that did it to him. The man who has often been accused of 'manipulating' his audience clearly found it easy to manipulate his own emotions, to the extent that, on finishing *Bohème*, he admitted that he had 'had to get up and, standing in the middle of the study, alone in the silence of the night, I began to weep like a child. It was as though I had seen my own child die.'

Yet the volatile directness of his emotions was such that, within a day or two, he was cavorting in fancy dress with a group of his Torre

When the rigours of composition were over, Puccini enjoyed enacting scenes from his operas with friends. He is photographed here at an improvised concert party celebrating the completion of *La bohème*.

del Lago cronies, pretending to be a Roman Emperor in the company of an admiral, a priest and a Turk – a bit like the four male characters in Act IV of his own opera, in fact. So much for the theory that Puccini was a cool and calculating composer who had no deep feelings of his own.

But apart from composing *La bohème*, what had he been doing between 1892 and the work's première in 1896? Keeping his eye on the progress of *Manon Lescaut* and other operas was one activity. In so doing, he visited Hamburg in 1892 and 1893, and got as far as Budapest in 1894. Keeping his eye – through the sights of a rifle – on the wildlife of Torre del Lago was another. In spite of his enthusiasm for the sport, it does seem that he was never more than a very moderate marksman. His own comments on his prowess should therefore be taken with a pinch of salt, as when, on accepting an invitation to go shooting with his friend, the Marchese Ginori (dedicatee of *La bohème*), he wrote: 'I will terrorize my adored palmipeds, which have long been panting for my murderous and infallible lead. Boom!' To know that he probably missed will come as a relief to those who regard his propensity for hunting as the less acceptable side of his character. Giulio Ricordi was clearly one of them. In a letter to the composer in the summer of 1893 he recommended to Puccini that he keep one eye on the gun-sight but his thoughts on *La bohème*. In another he predicted that Puccini would end up in prison, where, undistracted by water fowl, he could 'blast forth gun shots of melody'.

With *La bohème*'s première pending in Turin, however, Puccini had to deal with more important matters than shooting. The Teatro Regio, he knew, was well equipped to deal with the work's intricacies. It had recently been renovated, and had been fitted, on Toscanini's orders, with an orchestra pit and with a new lighting system that Puccini, too, thought to be necessary. As the first night on 1 February 1896 – three years to the day after the première of *Manon Lescaut* in the same surroundings – was scheduled to follow twenty-one hugely acclaimed performances of Wagner's *Götterdämmerung* (its Italian debut) and a production of Verdi's *Falstaff*, Puccini's nervousness was understandable. Since Elvira, significantly, did not go with him to provide moral support, we can trace the run-down to the opening night through his letters home, and in these, as usual, it is easy to sense his characteristic unease. On the one hand, he spoke optimistically of how he expected it to go. On the other, he admitted years later that he looked forward to the first night 'with the same joyous anticipation with which a prisoner walks to the scaffold'.

Yet with Cesira Ferrari ('good', according to Puccini) as Mimi and Camilla Pasini ('excellent') as Musetta, at least two of the leading roles seemed in safe hands. It was Ferrari who had portrayed Manon in the same surroundings three years earlier. Evan Gorga, as Rodolfo, was more of a handicap, his voice ('not so bad, but I doubt whether he will last') so overstretched that Puccini had to transpose down much of the tenor part for him. Completing the main quartet, Tieste Wilmant's Marcello was a further problem ('full of goodwill, but a terrible actor...in short out of place'). Quite apart from vocal quality, credible portrayals really mattered to Puccini. 'As you know,' he wrote to Elvira, 'this opera needs vivacious acting.'

In 1896 a composer of Puccini's calibre wielded more power than he would do now. He supervised the rehearsals himself, and insisted on precise co-ordination between sight and sound. His stage directions, just like Wagner's and Verdi's, were meticulous, and had to be observed. He followed the action down to the smallest detail. The slightest mishap, the tiniest piece of mistiming, could arouse his wrath. He knew how easily an effect could be destroyed by a curtain rising or dropping too soon. In the days before his operas fell into the hands of producers, Puccini's word was law. Only the conductor of *La bohème* spoke with anything like the composer's authority. That conductor being the rigorous Toscanini, he provided plenty of evidence for the composer's later description of him as 'un miracolo' ('a miracle').

So when the critics declared *La bohème* to be more 'trivial' than *Manon Lescaut* – one of them notoriously thought it would scarcely leave a mark on the history of opera – Puccini's worst fears seemed confirmed. Yet the work's sheer novelty value was bound to arouse suspicion. Nothing quite like it, in terms of pace and vivacious interplay, had been seen before. Its quick-changing moods, its juxtaposing of seriousness with frivolity, must have disconcerted its first-night audience. So must the fact that, in a supposedly sentimental opera, nobody – least of all Rodolfo – actually sees Mimi die, though everybody is in the room beside her. It is Schaunard the

Mimi's death scene from the 1899 Paris Opera production of *La bohème*. When Puccini finished composing this part of the opera, he said, 'I began to weep like a child. It was as though I had seen my own child die.'

musician, not her poetic lover, who suddenly notices what has happened. What was an audience meant to think?

Yet not everybody was hostile or uncomprehending, and the performance was a genuine occasion. 'At eight-thirty', reported one observer, 'most of the seats were occupied and the audience seemed eager.' The Duke and Duchess of Aosta were present. Mascagni and Ricordi were in the stalls. As Toscanini prepared to give the downbeat there was total silence. As the performance progressed, the good impressions grew, thanks to the scrupulously contrasted emotions, effectively expressed with the utmost melodic clarity. Mimì's death scene was heard with 'great attention and in total silence'. At the end, the audience rose to its feet...

Princess Letizia of Piemonte, who was there, invited Puccini into her box for Act III (an honour, it is said, that deeply embarrassed him). Had Toscanini not enforced Turin's strict 'no encore' regime, or had there been someone easier-going in the pit, 'Che gelida manina' ('Your tiny hand is frozen') would surely have been encored and Puccini would have been asked to take a bow, thus adding to the lustre, if not the continuity, of the evening.

But at least, at the end, the composer enjoyed five curtain calls, and the critic of the *Corriere della Sera* was right in predicting – as almost nobody else did – that the opera would have a long future. Before long, in sheet-music form, Rodolfo's 'Che gelida manina', Mimì's 'Sì, mi chiamano Mimì', and Musetta's Waltz Song would all be internationally marketed for domestic performance. Meanwhile, with idyllic memories of *Manon Lescaut*'s thirty curtain calls in the same theatre, Puccini drew cold comfort from *La bohème*'s seemingly more modest success. In his own characteristically self-pitying words, he returned to his hotel completely heartbroken. 'There was within me sadness, melancholy, a wish to cry.'

But even while working on *La bohème*, as well as immediately afterwards, Puccini had been shrewdly looking ahead and beginning to devise his next work – which suggests that he may have been thicker-skinned about criticism than he often seemed. Whatever his doubts, something inside him made him aware that his career as an opera composer was progressing. He knew that *La bohème* was a masterpiece, and that it would soon establish itself – which, within a year or two, it did. Productions were staged in, among other places,

Rome, Palermo, Buenos Aires, Moscow, Vienna, New York, Los
Angeles, Athens, London, and Paris itself, where Debussy, by no
means one of Puccini's more ardent admirers, told the Spanish
composer, Manuel de Falla, that he could think of nobody who had
portrayed nineteenth-century Paris better than Puccini.

For the first production in Naples, Puccini went as far as to
nominate Arthur Nikisch, celebrated Brahmsian and conductor of the
Berlin Philharmonic, to follow in Toscanini's footsteps. This was not
the act of a composer uncertain of his genius, though it prompted
Giulio Ricordi to quiver with horror at the thought of a foreigner
conducting in an Italian theatre. It would, he said, 'result in a *dies
irae*', or day of wrath. Puccini did not get his way. But he made sure
that, in his now established role as watchdog, he travelled with his
opera almost wherever it went – even to Manchester ('A veritable
inferno! A horrible place to stay!'), though Paris must have proved
scarcely more appealing, if the homesick letter he wrote to a friend in
Lucca was anything to go by.

The work he now had on his mind – it had been there as far back
as *Manon Lescaut* if not earlier – was *Tosca*. At first it had seemed a
hopeless task. Though the subject, incorporating sex and sadism,
was inviting, and though its degree of 'realism' seemed about right
for a composer who was never wholly committed to the more
crudely realistic trend in Italian opera at that time, Puccini found
himself faced with a problem he had not previously encountered: the
need to get a living playwright's permission to transform one of his
plays into an opera. Victorien Sardou, Paris-based author of *Tosca*,
withheld that right. Perhaps, to begin with, he had never heard of
the upstart Italian who wanted to grab his play away from him;
perhaps he felt as indifferent as Goethe did when sent a copy of his
poem *Erlkönig* set to music by an unknown young Viennese
composer called Franz Schubert.

At any rate, as early as 1892, Sardou had sent word that he disliked
Puccini's music (it was doubtful that he even knew a note of it) and
did not want *Tosca* tampered with. Puccini thereupon typically backed
away from the idea, and briefly turned his attention to Maeterlinck's
Pelléas et Mélisande, a play that approached sex and sadism from a
different, but no less promising, angle. What he might have made of it
would be a fascinating subject for a thesis, and provides a reminder of

how astute Puccini was at finding subjects that suited him. Filled with enthusiasm, he visited the playwright in Belgium but found to his chagrin that the play had already been promised to Debussy.

Stonewalled by both playwrights – though evidently with deep regret by Maeterlinck, who, one suspects, would have preferred Puccini to Debussy as composer of *Pelléas* – he might then have abandoned both projects. A plan to base an opera on a Zola novel similarly foundered (Massenet had moved faster). But something about *Tosca* continued to entice him, to the extent that for the one and only time in his career he revived a project he had previously dropped.

In the meantime, however, Puccini's prospects of capturing *Tosca* had not improved. The play had by then been promised to a fellow Italian composer, Alberto Franchetti, and Illica – in the belief that Puccini had lost interest – had gone as far as to write a libretto, with Ricordi's blessing. Even the octogenarian Verdi, in a valedictory sort of way, had got in on the act by saying that, of all Sardou's plays, *Tosca* was the one he himself would have liked to transform into an opera. Visiting Sardou in Paris, Italy's senior composer timed his arrival to coincide with Illica's reading of his proposed libretto to the playwright. Bestowing his approval, he paid special tribute to the poetic 'farewell to art and life' that Illica had written for the tenor hero, Cavaradossi, before his execution by firing squad in the last act.

Puccini (right), pictured at the keyboard with two of his rivals, Pietro Mascagni (left), and Alberto Franchetti (centre). Franchetti had gained the rights for *Tosca* but relinquished them when Puccini told him it would be a bad subject for an opera.

Was it cussedness or his own keen theatrical instinct that prompted Puccini to delete that passage from the libretto when *Tosca* ultimately came his way? Verdi may have been sufficiently moved by it to seize the manuscript from Illica's hand and – so the story goes – read the lines aloud in a quavering voice, but Puccini knew that long poetic farewells could disastrously hold up the action of that sort of operatic melodrama.

How Puccini finally gained access to *Tosca* seemed at the time even more devious than his acquisition of *La bohème* was reputed to be, and as self-interested as any unscrupulous act perpetrated by Wagner. In brief, Puccini – with Ricordi as his mouthpiece – persuaded the moderately gifted but clearly thoroughly gullible composer Franchetti that *Tosca* was a truly bad subject for an opera. Its plot, he pointed out, was unsavoury, its action brutal, its emphasis on rape, murder, and execution would dismay audiences everywhere. Franchetti – who had already given up composing *Andrea Chénier*, an assignment that finally went to the young Umberto Giordano – thanked Ricordi for his thoughtful advice and willingly relinquished the rights. Ricordi immediately signed up Puccini to compose *Tosca*. Recent research, throwing more favourable light on Puccini's and Ricordi's crookedness, has challenged the conspiracy theory by claiming that Franchetti 'wearied' of the *Tosca* project four months before Ricordi urged Puccini to reconsider composing the opera.

But there was one more stumbling block, and that was Giacosa, whose poetry – as an ingredient of *Tosca's* libretto – was as vital as Illica's prose. The trouble was that Giacosa detested Sardou's play, and said so in no uncertain terms, firing off an explosive letter to Ricordi about its 'absolute inadaptability' to the musical stage. Sweepingly deriding the project, he asserted that 'The first act consists of nothing but duets. Nothing but duets in the second act, except for the short torture scene in which only two characters are seen on the stage. The third act is one interminable duet.'

How Puccini eventually solved what could, as Giacosa diagnosed, have been a very real problem is an object-lesson in the workings of genius. And although Giacosa – Illica shared his views but proved more equable – constantly threatened to withdraw from what he considered could only be a 'calamity', the three men (with Ricordi as usual in support) thrashed out an opera among them that vanquished

Giacosa's doubts. Its police-state story, unfolded with relentless tension, is a thriller of a sort no other composer could have handled with Puccini's assurance: in it, the artist Cavaradossi helps a political prisoner to escape, only to find that he has inadvertently placed himself and his beloved Tosca in the clutches of the evil police chief Scarpia.

Based as it was on a stage play powered by the clash of personalities, Puccini's *Tosca* naturally made much of the duets about which Giacosa had been so outspoken. It was not a work whose success depended on big ensembles. When Illica proposed a quartet for the torture scene, Puccini instantly squashed it. In fact, far from stifling the work, the duets – not quite so 'interminable' as Giacosa feared – merely form part of an ever-changing dramatic fabric in which the fates of a brave young actress, a subversive painter, and a brutal chief of police are relentlessly interwoven.

There are aspects of *Tosca* – in its emphasis on freedom, tyranny and the horrors of political imprisonment – that resemble the plot of Beethoven's *Fidelio*. But Puccini's heroine, by bribing the sadistic Scarpia with her body and then by killing him, goes further than Beethoven's Leonore ever needs to (or, by the composer, would ever have been allowed to) in order to save the life of her beloved Florestan from the hands of a cruel and determined adversary. It is significant that in *Fidelio* the couple are man and wife, whereas in *Tosca* they are lovers. It is notable, too, that at the end of *Fidelio* the principal characters are all still alive, whereas at the end of *Tosca* they are all dead.

Puccini's music, dating from a later point in the nineteenth century, is consistently more violent and more explicit than Beethoven's, which sustains, with the help of its text, a high moral tone that is irrelevant to Puccini's drama. Puccini was never a visionary in the Beethovenian sense, and politics mattered infinitely less to him than to Beethoven. But that is not to say that *Tosca* is simply coarse. True, it is one of his most masculine works, and its attitudes can seem repellent. When, in 1898, Puccini was beginning to think about the opera's première, he asked Toscanini if he would be prepared to conduct it. 'Remember, you must be the one to deflower her.' It was an opportunity Toscanini eventually declined.

Yet it is a score that contains 'Vissi d'arte' ('Love and music, these I have lived for'), one of Puccini's greatest feminine arias of despair,

The cover of the original Ricordi edition of *Tosca*, showing the heroine placing a crucifix on the body of Scarpia after she has stabbed him to death at the climax of Act Two

along with two of his most eloquent tenor arias, the artist hero's 'Recondita armonia' ('Strange harmony of contrasts') and 'E lucevan le stelle' ('The stars were shining brightly'), sung on the roof of Rome's Castel Sant'Angelo on the dawn of his execution day. Scarpia's lustful voicing of his Credo, which coincides with a choral Te Deum in the Church of Sant'Andrea della Valle at the end of Act I, is a brilliant *coup de théâtre* of a sort only Puccini (or perhaps Verdi) could have devised. Thereafter, with all the composer's sureness of pace, the torturing of Cavaradossi, the attempted rape of Tosca, her murder of Scarpia, her lover's execution scene and her final distraught leap from the battlements – with the orchestral picture of dawn over Rome as a soft and exquisite interlude amid the mayhem – are hurled at us with a relish firmly based on the principle that too much is not enough.

These, admittedly, are aspects of *Tosca* that bring the audience searingly close to the action, thereby prompting the American scholar and critic, Joseph Kerman, to dismiss Puccini's opera as 'that shabby little shocker'. The phrase has gone down in operatic history, even though Bernard Shaw had already used something very like it when he called Sardou's play 'that turnip head of a cheap shocker'. Of course, compared with the more tender and convivial *La bohème*, *Tosca* is indeed a shocker. That, after all, is what Puccini meant it to be. The fact that it has stood the test of time, giving Sardou a durability he did not deserve and and surviving a limitless number of performances, shows the extent of its success. To complain that its popularity has blocked the progress of other, perhaps more deserving, operas sounds like the sour grapes with which Puccini's sheer expertise has always been greeted.

Treated with the attention it deserves, *Tosca* will always be an arresting work. More than that, it will demonstrate that the title-role – Tosca is in fact her surname, Floria her first name – provides considerable scope for subtlety. At the same time, as a bludgeoning study of political unrest, of the corruption of power, and of artists expressing their feelings then being brutally punished for doing so, it is as horrifyingly truthful today – think of recent events in Nigeria – as it was in 1900.

That is why, of all Puccini's operas, it is the one that can be updated most easily and effectively, even if the action was placed by the composer very positively in the year 1800. Puccini was no politician. His lack of political awareness, perhaps of any ability whatsoever to think in any constructive political way, suggests that he was unlikely to have considered the work to be a cautionary tale, applicable to any period in history. The *New Grove Dictionary of Opera* bluntly calls his handling of this element in *Tosca* 'inept'. But as with his pictures of Paris in *La bohème*, he set early nineteenth-century Rome in the most precise focus. He expected his stage directions to be carried out to the letter, and would have been furious had they not been. A good new production of *Tosca* in Puccini's lifetime – and there were plenty of these – was one that looked like a perfected version of the one before.

To update or otherwise adjust a work so absolutely cut and dried would have seemed to him an invasion of his composer's rights. Yet a number of modern productions have done so, not only Jonathan Miller's in London but, before that, Anthony Besch's justly famous Scottish Opera version, with Mussolini and little King Vittorio Emanuele parading through the Church of Sant' Andrea della Valle in Act I, with Tosca dressed like someone out of *Roma, Città Aperta*, and with a prostitute in Scarpia's camp-bed in Act II. Such glosses on *Tosca* have demonstrated how easily it can be transformed into the equivalent of a film by Roberto Rosselini or a novel by Alberto Moravia. Cavaradossi's cry of victory on hearing that Napoleon had defeated the Austrians at the Battle of Marengo may be in these circumstances hard to explain – it was as well, one critic remarked, that the performance was not sung in English translation – but this seemed a small price to pay for the immediacy of the rest of the performance.

Puccini's long-term enthusiasm for *Tosca* as a potential subject for an opera had lured him to Florence as early as 1895 in order to see Sarah Bernhardt in the Sardou play. He did not think much of her, deeming her portrayal so 'lifeless' that he began to fear the play itself was at fault. Was this something really worth transforming into an opera? Expressing his disappointment to Ricordi, he was reassured to hear that Bernhardt had been unwell in Florence and that in Milan she had performed 'with fire'.

Only Giacosa's misgivings about the plot then stood in his way, but as work progressed even these began to dwindle. Most of the customary hold-ups by this point were being caused by Puccini's own travels around Europe to observe the progress of *La bohème* during the last years of the nineteenth century. Nevertheless he had some time to himself in Tuscany, and a trip to Rome was justified by the need to hear how the city's church bells would sound from the top of the Castel Sant'Angelo, where the opera's denouement was to take place. The great bell of St Peter's, as he discovered to his pleasure, struck a low E, a sonority he was able to interweave with other bell effects and with the offstage voice of a distant shepherd boy. These, between them, would atmospherically enhance the orchestra's short prelude to Act III, Puccini's evocation of the Roman dawn before Cavaradossi's execution.

Following page, Anthony Besch's famous 1980 production of Tosca for Scottish Opera updated the setting to Mussolini's Italy. This photograph of the end of Act One shows Marina Krilovici, her back to the camera, in the title role, and Guillermo Sarabia's jack-booted Scarpia at the left. Standing around Tosca are Mussolini and King Vittorio Emanuele.

LA TOSCA
Sarah Bernhardt
(3ᵐᵉ Costume)

MARIO
(Dumény)

Sarah Bernhardt as Tosca in Sardou's play in the late 1880s. Puccini saw her in the role in Florence in 1895, five years before the première of his opera, but found her so 'lifeless' that he began to fear the play was at fault.

The exactitude Puccini brought to his picture of Rome remains a special feature of the opera, and in recent years it inspired one distinguished Italian director to film a version of *Tosca* making use of the actual settings where the action takes place. But the real authenticity lies in the music. Even the melody of the Te Deum in Act I was tracked down for Puccini by one of his Roman contacts, and the cantata sung offstage by Tosca in the Palazzo Farnese (Scarpia's headquarters adjoining the Campo de'Fiori, now the French Embassy past which tourists now tread daily) at the start of Act II was a deft pastiche by Puccini of music by the eighteenth-century composer, Giovanni Paisiello, who was his grandfather's teacher in Naples and who sided with Napoleon in 1799.

When a composer goes to such pains to get things right, it is understandable that he expects no less of his librettists and even of the playwright on whose work he bases his opera. One of Sardou's few suggestions to Puccini was that Tosca's death-leap from the battlements of the Castel Sant'Angelo, with St Peter's in the background, should end in the River Tiber below. On being told that the river flowed past the other side of the castle, he accused Puccini – to the composer's irritation – of unnecessary fussiness.

Puccini finally produced exactly the work he had wanted to write. No concessions of any importance had had to be made, and only one opportunity had been missed – the chance to end the opera, exactly as it began, with the series of exultant chords that depicted the brutal Scarpia even before he appeared on stage. Were they to be ironically hammered out by the orchestra as the curtain falls, these same chords would suggest Scarpia to be posthumously gloating over the fate of Tosca and Cavaradossi. Instead, as Joseph Kerman has cynically pointed out, Puccini got the orchestra to 'scream the first thing that comes into its head' – that being the melody of Cavaradossi's aria, 'E lucevan le stelle', from the start of Act III. But would the audience have grasped the implications of Scarpia's motif if it were played at the close of the opera? Perhaps they would. But the music which most people have always associated with *Tosca* is that of 'E lucevan le stelle', and Puccini could be said to have been instinctively correct, though not necessarily subtle, to end the work in the way in which he did.

The score of *Tosca* – though today's opponents of the composer naturally accuse it of opportunistic backwardness – contained some forward-looking features. Scarpia's blatant chords were based on notes of the whole-tone scale, which Debussy had pioneered in his concert works but would not employ operatically until two years later. Their stark ferocity also anticipated the music of Strauss's *Salome* and *Elektra*, which were not written until 1905 and 1909 respectively. In this way, *Tosca* not only reflected but even anticipated the temper of a decade that would ultimately produce Schoenberg's nightmarish *Erwartung* (the first performance of which was delayed until 1924) and most of Mahler's symphonies. Béla Bartók's psychodrama, *Duke*

Opposite, a page from the manuscript of *Tosca*. Puccini's handwritten musical scores, with their scribbled amendments, grew no tidier as he matured.

Bluebeard's Castle, would follow in 1911 and, in 1921, Berg's *Wozzeck*, a subject that might well have attracted Puccini on account of its sado-masochistic subject matter and the personality of the down-trodden Marie.

In spite of Giacosa's prolonged grumbling, the completion of *Tosca* was, by Puccini's standards, fairly painless. The fierce directness and conciseness of the piece prevented him from having quite so many of his usual second thoughts and self-doubts, even in the face of Ricordi's demoralizing belief that the central duet between Tosca and Cavaradossi in the last act was unacceptably long and sub-standard. But then, Ricordi had been expecting Puccini – on the strength of Verdi's professional advice – to provide a heroic 'Hymn to Life and Art' at that point, and found, to his disappointment, that Puccini had rejected the idea. Hymns to life and art were much more Verdi's or Berlioz's line than Puccini's, and he was surely right to accept the fact and to produce, instead, exactly what was needed in the circumstances: a recognition of Cavaradossi's predicament, and of his despair, just before being shot.

Ricordi, admittedly, was additionally aware – and greatly displeased – that Puccini had artfully revamped some discarded music from *Edgar* as part of the duet. The composer, however, argued forcefully that he used this music not merely as an expedient, because it was there, but because it possessed the correct poetic spirit. Moreover, since Ricordi had yet to see the manuscript of the impressionistic orchestral prelude to the act, which considerably altered its structure, he had only a rough idea of what the finished product would be like. Puccini's will-power proved the stronger, and *Tosca* was duly presented on 14 January 1900 at the Teatro Costanzi in Rome – an adroit choice of location for so thoroughly Roman a work, even if only a small part of the large audience guessed itself to be in the presence of what was destined to be one of the most popular operas ever written.

But then, their attention was by all accounts divided between the performance and what seems to have been the supercharged atmosphere of the Rome auditorium that night. Fears that anti-Puccini, anti-Milan and anti-Turin factions would be in the audience, intent on disrupting the performance, may have proved groundless, but an accompanying bomb threat had to be taken seriously, particularly as Queen Margherita had been invited to attend.

The conductor was advised that, in the event of trouble, he should stop the performance and switch to the National Anthem. Hardly had the opera begun when the inevitable happened. A mob of late-comers, mistaken for anarchists, set the audience in an uproar. The panic-stricken conductor, who had survived an earlier bomb explosion in a different theatre, fled from the pit. Somehow calm was restored and the performance restarted. The Queen (whose husband, ironically, was assassinated a few months later) arrived in time for Act II. In spite of the distractions, most of the opera's big moments – including Cavaradossi's two arias, the Te Deum and Tosca's prayer – were acclaimed, and even the long Act III duet (about which Ricordi had expressed such doubts) held the audience in its grip. The critics were in disarray, but the *Corriere d'Italia*, at least, got its priorities right. On its front page was a full-scale serious review of the opera rather than a sensational report of the events of the night.

Certainly the disturbance had done nothing to sabotage Puccini's opera. With the elegant Romanian soprano, Hariclea Darclée, as Tosca, the title-role was in reliable hands: she had already shown her qualities in productions of *Manon Lescaut* and *La bohème*, and she combined an impressive stage presence with beauty of tone. The composer even managed to justify what now seems a perverse decision to choose Emilio de Marchi as Cavaradossi rather than Enrico Caruso. But Caruso – who, as a tenor in residence at the Teatro Costanzi that year, was not only available but had expected to be given the role – was not yet Italy's most adulated singer, and Puccini knew De Marchi's acting ability and vocal technique to be (at that time) superior. 'Caruso,' claimed Puccini, 'won't learn anything. He's lazy and he's too pleased with himself.' As for Eugenio Giraldoni, whose repertoire included Boris Godunov, Hans Sachs and Eugene Onegin, he was chosen just as carefully. Though deemed by some to be too sadistic a Scarpia, he was not just any old Italian baritone. He brought ample authority to the part, and proved again how astute Puccini's selection of singers could be, and how he expected them to be able actors as well.

Good acting, indeed, was by then becoming a vital ingredient of opera performances in Italy. No longer was it enough for a singer simply to stand and deliver, and it was thanks partly to Puccini's attention to the fine detail of his operas that this had come about. So

Below, Hariclea Darclée as Tosca, one of the roles she created. The Romanian soprano combined a mag-netic stage presence with an impressive vocal technique.

Far right, Emilio de Marchi, Puccini's choice for the role of Cavaradossi in *Tosca* (much to Caruso's disappointment)

theatrically explicit was the action of *Tosca* that there was a real necessity to get it right. Not only was Puccini himself on hand to oversee the rehearsals but so was Giulio Ricordi's thirty-one-year-old son Tito who, though trained as an engineer, was showing an increasing (and some would say interfering) interest in how Puccini's operas were staged.

Taking personal charge of the production, Tito showed himself to be a new sort of director – volatile, arrogant, dedicated, irritating, and thus perhaps similar to some of his modern counterparts. Puccini, who was destined to clash with him in later years, seemed as yet to be unperturbed by his demands, though there were strong objections in Rome to the decision to appoint a German Milanese designer, Adolfo von Hohenstein, for the *Tosca* décor. But since Hohenstein had already designed the original *Manon Lescaut* and *La bohème* (as well as the première production of Verdi's *Falstaff*), his work must have been to Puccini's taste. His *Tosca* sets, indeed, were to prove the prototype for all but the most outlandish modern presentations of the opera.

Darclée and Giraldoni reappeared in the work's Scala première three months later, when the thirty-three-year-old Arturo Toscanini – too late to perform the deflowering ceremony promised to him by the composer – took over from Leopoldo Mugnone, the Teatro Costanzi's much admired resident conductor (Sir Thomas Beecham thought him the best in Italy, though Puccini came to consider him 'flabby'). Giuseppe Borgatti, Milan's distinguished Wagnerian *Heldentenor*, replaced De Marchi as Cavaradossi.

At La Scala, in spite of having Toscanini at the helm, *Tosca*'s reception was as mixed as it had been in Rome. The Milanese audience, always as good as the Milanese critics at cutting people down to size, thought Puccini had grown too big for his boots, and not until Darclée reached 'Vissi d'arte' did the ice begin to melt. All the same, *Tosca* moved rapidly to London, New York and Paris, and Caruso was entrusted with the role of Cavaradossi at the Metropolitan Opera, New York. Meanwhile, with *Tosca*'s international future seemingly assured, Puccini could begin thinking about his next opera, the initially much more troublesome *Madama Butterfly*.

Though it marked the completion of his brilliant turn-of-the-century hat trick, *Butterfly* gave Puccini more heartache than either *La bohème* or *Tosca*. As usual, it took him time to find a subject. An opera based on the comic exploits of Alphonse Daudet's Tartarin – a Provençal combination of Don Quixote and Sancho Panza – was discussed with Illica but soon rejected. During his visit to London for the British première of *Tosca* at Covent Garden, however, he happened to see a short American play by David Belasco called *Madam Butterfly*. Although he spoke almost no English, he grasped the gist of the drama and admired the way it was staged. The stillness of Butterfly's ten-minute vigil, as she hopefully awaited her husband's return, awakened all his operatic instincts, as also, inevitably, did her subsequent suicide.

Much later, Belasco was to report – with what sounds like theatrical exaggeration – that Puccini had rushed up to him after the performance, weeping copiously, and asking if he could have the operatic rights to his play. Puccini could indeed be emotional, but it seems likely, on this occasion, that he was more prudent than that. En route for home, he visited Émile Zola – a man who, with his emphasis on misery and misfortune, might be described in some ways as Puccini's literary equivalent – in Paris to discuss the possiblity of making an opera out of one of his novels. Dostoyevsky's autobiographical memoir, *From the House of the Dead*, also claimed his attention, but was deemed too awkward to transform into an opera – though his Czechoslovakian contemporary, Leoš Janáček, eventually did so. Then, not for the first time, he considered an opera on the subject of Marie Antoinette. Clearly, the idea of *Madama Butterfly* was not yet firmly fixed in his mind. Nevertheless *Madama Butterfly* was what it was to be. By the end of a year that had begun with the almost explosive première of *Tosca*, he had written to Giulio Ricordi in

Émile Zola, the distinguished French novelist, whom Puccini visited in Paris in the hope, never fulfilled, that they might collaborate on an opera

Milan, declaring his interest in the 'irresistible' Japanese heroine. Not
for another three years, however, would the sad life and death of
Madama Butterfly be finally pinned down by Puccini.

During that time, Italy's operatic life seemed increasingly moribund.
Verdi's long reign as Italy's leading composer ended with his death in
1901, Mascagni's inspiration lay dormant in the wake of *Le maschere*
and Giordano's in the wake of *Fedora*, neither work proving of any
long-term consequence. Leoncavallo slid into the world of operetta.
Boito continued to wrestle with his never-to-be-finished *Nerone*.
Respighi had yet to establish himself. Compared with what the
influential Debussy was doing in France, Mahler in Austria, Richard
Strauss in Germany, and Schoenberg in Germany and Austria, Italian
soil at the start of the twentieth century seemed depressingly infertile.
Only Puccini managed to flourish in it as a composer of significance,
and to keep his name actively before the public.

A sensational production of *Tosca* at Bologna in 1900 had certainly
done that, with Caruso as Cavaradossi at last persuading the composer
that he was the right man for the role. Yet offering the stocky
Neapolitan, as his reward for perseverance, the chance to make his

Enrico Caruso as
Cavaradossi in Act One of
Tosca. He finally appeared
in the role in a production
in Bologna, in the same
year as the work's Rome
première in January 1900.

Scala début in a revival of *La bohème* under Toscanini's conductorship once again antagonized the Milanese public against Puccini. Having just been denied a new production of Wagner's *Tristan*, which they wanted to see, they were in no mood for another *Bohème*, even with Caruso as Rodolfo.

As a result, the first night was received with what was said to be 'fatal silence'. Puccini retreated to Torre del Lago to inflict his wrath on the wildlife, but was soon back in Milan in January 1901 for Verdi's funeral, at which he was the City of Lucca's official representative. Verdi, aged eighty-seven, had lain unconscious for a week at the Grand Hotel et de Milan, along the road from La Scala. Traffic had been rerouted and tram-drivers told not to clang their bells. Daily bulletins had been hung at the hotel's entrance, giving details of the dying octogenarian's heart and respiration rates. Could the forty-three-year-old Puccini, who had become Italy's leading composer overnight, hope for similar consideration when his own time came? If Puccini thought of it, as he doubtless did, it could only have been with dismay. Death – his own death – was something for which he maintained a superstitious horror.

Caruso's decisive Scala success in Gaetano Donizetti's long familiar *L'Elisir d'amore* a fortnight later, however, must have made him wonder about whether he would ever be considered Verdi's successor. So must the piece of gossip he received from Illica that the Milanese public thought him 'lazy'. But this, at least, spurred him into action over *Madama Butterfly*.

By March he had sent Illica an Italian translation of the crudely-written short story by John Luther Long, a Philadelphian lawyer, on which Belasco had based his play. Apprehensive about Illica's reaction, Puccini advised him that the play was better than the story. But Illica, who immediately saw the potential for a great deal of beautiful music, was so impressed by the story of the vulnerable Japanese geisha-girl, who abandons her national traditions to marry a feckless American sailor, that he started sketching a libretto right away – unperturbed by the fact that the original story ended startlingly differently, with Butterfly's little hilltop house standing deserted when the duplicitous Lieutenant Pinkerton returns to it from America with his new wife, and with Butterfly by then living elsewhere in Nagasaki.

The crowds of mourners on the day of Verdi's funeral in January 1901 brought Milan to a standstill. Puccini attended the ceremony of his illustrious compatriot as the city of Lucca's official representative.

Illica was uncertain, however, about how someone as 'unsympathetic' as Pinkerton could be transformed into the opera's leading tenor. He communicated his doubts to Ricordi, whose response, Puccini discovered, was 'somewhat cold' to the whole idea of the opera. But then, Ricordi's information, like Illica's, was based misleadingly on John Luther Long's inept story, not on Belasco's much more professional play. Some of the opera's subsequent structural problems may well have begun at this point. Its long succession of delays certainly did, because three months passed before Illica finally received an Italian translation of the Belasco version. As Puccini expected, he was instantly bowled over by it. So, too, was Ricordi, who confessed that he could not sleep for thinking about it.

Changing attitudes, of course, were nothing new when plans for a Puccini opera were in their early stages. And though Puccini, Illica and Ricordi were by now in what seemed reasonable accord, the increasingly touchy Giacosa had still to be reckoned with. By the time he entered the discussions, in 1902, he was in poor health – he died four years later – and grumbled that Puccini was doing nothing but nag him. Giacosa, in consequence, nagged Ricordi, and Puccini himself was nagged by Elvira, with whom he had been living by then for twenty years, with still no wedding in prospect. Elvira's estranged husband, alas, remained stubbornly alive in Lucca. Her daughter,

Fosca, had recently married and gone off to Milan. She herself, at the vulnerable age of forty-two, suspected that she was being ostracized by Puccini's posh friends, felt increasingly neglected by Puccini himself, and feared that she might be replaced at any moment by one or another of the young admirers who surrounded him constantly.

Prosperity, indeed, was now conspicuously changing Puccini's life. Along with Maurice Ravel in France, he was one of the first famous composers to discover the excitement of motoring, and his fast cars (fast, at least, by the standards of the day) were just another source of worry and disgruntlement for Elvira. As priorities in his life, they stood below music but considerably higher than she herself did – or so she thought. Moreover, and worse, they gave him the freedom to roam and to display the fact that he could afford a chauffeur-driven limousine. Ironically, however, she was in the vehicle with him one night in 1902 when, after dinner with his old friend, the café owner,

Puccini recovering from the motoring accident in 1902 that left him with a permanent limp. His lengthy convalescence, during which it was discovered that he was suffering from diabetes, plunged him into a state of deep melancholy.

Puccini at the wheel of his
cherished 24 horse-power
La Buire, parked outside his
villa at Torre del Lago

Alfredo Caselli, in Lucca, the car went over an embankment and hit a tree.

Though Elvira emerged unscathed, Puccini himself suffered a serious fracture in his right leg. The damaged limb, over-hastily set, had to be rebroken later. His convalescence, complicated by the discovery that he was suffering from diabetes, took several months and plunged him into a state of deep melancholy. 'Goodbye to everything, goodbye to Butterfly, goodbye to life', he told Illica, somewhat histrionically. His spirits were not raised by a letter from Ricordi, tactlessly telling him that he could have been 'the modern Rossini' but was at risk of becoming no more than 'the unhappy Donizetti'. Ricordi did not spell out the implication of his remark, but the forty-four-year-old Puccini was bound to deduce that it referred to Donizetti's death at the age of fifty-one, paralysed by syphilis.

The letter, whatever its intentions, did not galvanize Puccini into action. *Madama Butterfly* drifted rather than raced towards completion. He feared that Act I was going to be too long – his fears later proved right – and that the two scenes of Act II might similarly stretch the audience's patience. To console himself he bought a new car, a Lancia, but this failed to cheer him up as much as he hoped. 'My life,' he told Illica, 'is a sea of sadness and I am stuck with it.'

In such a mood he found himself identifying so strongly with the fate of his little Japanese heroine that, as had already happened with *La bohème*, he could hardly bear to finish the score. His abiding desire to monitor the progress of his earlier operas – which even after his leg injury still enabled him to make regular escapes from Elvira and enjoy his little flings – made inroads on his time. The Paris première of *Tosca*, which he attended in person, caused one such interruption, though its outcome seemed par for the course. Loved by the audience, it was loathed by the critics. Around this time, in 1903, even the news that Elvira's husband had died came to seem a mixed blessing. Though it enabled them at last to marry – on home ground at Torre del Lago – and though it meant that their eighteen-year-old son Antonio could now legitimately become a Puccini, it did nothing to improve their shaky relationship. Indeed, as soon became apparent, it did the opposite.

With *Madama Butterfly* due to open at La Scala, on 17 February 1904, the 'official' reading of the libretto to members of the cast took

Outside his villa at Torre del Lago, Puccini reads a newspaper, while his wife Elvira and son Antonio stare unsmilingly at the camera.

place perilously late – by today's standards at any rate – in the middle of January. To Giacosa, in his capacity as Puccini's poet, went the honour of declaiming the lines from the stage of the opera house. The singers were given their parts in proof form, page by page, and told not to take them home, because of Ricordi's perpetual fear that they might fall into the wrong hands (this was more likely to be a form of publicity seeking). Although Puccini was present to make corrections, there was scant time for much in the way of modification. Postponement, in Milan of all places, could have spelt doom.

But since, as things turned out, the Milan production was doomed anyway, postponement might have been the wiser course. Puccini himself, bearing in mind his previous experiences in the most famous of all opera houses, should have been alert enough to see danger ahead, even if he failed to visualize the scale of the forthcoming disaster. Yet though there was uncertainty backstage as to whether the work should be performed in two acts or three – a problem that has persisted to this day – nobody admitted the possibility of failure. In most respects, after all, the omens were good. The twenty-eight-year-old Rosina Storchio, who was Puccini's charming, light-voiced choice for the title-role, had already been a hit as Musetta in *La bohème*. She had sung Manon, had been Toscanini's Gretel in Engelbert Humperdinck's *Hänsel und Gretel*, and was held in high regard. Giovanni Zenatello, the equally youthful Pinkerton, was a reliable

Rosina Storchio, Puccini's
choice for the title role in
Madama Butterfly at La
Scala, Milan in 1904. After
the débâcle of the opening
night Puccini admitted that
she might have been too
'doll-like' for the part.

tenor, considered indeed to be one of La Scala's most promising
acquisitions. And to have Giuseppe De Luca, at the start of his long
and successful career, as the sympathetic American consul Sharpless,
who tries unsuccessfully to explain to Butterfly that her husband is a
boor, could only have been a bonus.

So what went wrong? Apart from the revelation of the work's
structural problems, there was the fact, quite simply, that many people
in Milan wanted Puccini to fail. He was not the Scala audience's
favourite composer. He was a victim of rival factions – particularly of

Although Giovanni Zenatello in the original 1904 production of *Madama Butterfly* wore a dark uniform for the role of Pinkerton, a white summer look as pictured here soon became fashionable. Not many of today's exponents of Sharpless, the American Consul, would wear the upturned hat of the kind worn in this photograph.

Following page, the original stage set for the 1904 production of Madama Butterfly

people who supported Mascagni or felt Puccini's works to stand in the way of staging Wagner – as well as a good deal of bad-mouthing. His vanity, it was thought, needed to be fed a portion of humble pie. The behaviour of Giulio Ricordi, as Puccini's publisher, was considered equally high-handed. Conditions were right for an act of revenge. The absence of Toscanini as conductor – he had walked out of La Scala the previous year over the audience's incessant demand for encores – meant that a tolerant but adequate routinier, the forty-four-year-old Cleofonte Campanini, would be in the pit.

Almost from the start of *Madama Butterfly*'s first performance the audience made its hostility noisily plain. Yet La Scala itself had worked hard, and spent lavishly, on the opera's behalf. To achieve real delicacy of design, the distinguished Parisian stage painter, Lucien Jusseaume, had been brought in to realize Puccini's vision of 'A hill near Nagasaki; in the foreground a Japanese house with terrace and garden'. So evocative was the resultant stage picture that subsequent designers departed from its essential features – house on the left, landscape on the right – at their peril. To set *Madama Butterfly* in a grim tenement building, as one modern production has done, thus carries considerable shock value.

Tito Ricordi, his appetite whetted by *Tosca*, was again the director, determined to create a visual equivalent of the finesse of Puccini's music. Rehearsals went well. Puccini, who claimed to have poured into *Madama Butterfly* all his 'heart and soul', was happy, at least for the moment. The orchestral players, deeply impressed with the fastidious beauty and intensity of their music, stood up to acclaim the composer at the close of the dress rehearsal. To his star soprano, Puccini sent a message: 'My good wishes are unnecessary! The public will certainly be overpowered by your great art! And I hope, through you, to speed to victory.' So confident was he, all of a sudden, that he even permitted members of his own family (including one of his sisters and his son Antonio) to attend the first night. Never before, he admitted, would he have been willing to 'expose them to the uncertainty' of such an event.

Yet it all went wrong. The Milan public was not overpowered. Every resemblance to *La bohème* – particularly Butterfly's entrance music, which Puccini later altered – was loudly seized upon by the audience and catcalled. When the composer, still limping from his car accident, came in front of the curtain at the end of Act I, he was greeted with laughter. In Act II, not even the exquisite 'Un bel dì vedremo' ('One fine day') turned the tide in Puccini's favour. It, too, was mocked. When the curtain finally fell, there was total silence, shattered only by the sound of Pietro Mascagni, Puccini's old rival, weeping loudly and haranguing the audience for its disgraceful behaviour. But with Mascagni as a friend, Puccini might have remarked, who needed enemies?

Compared with the run of twenty performances *Tosca* had received in Rome, *Madama Butterfly* survived only one single terrible night in

Milan. Puccini's astute publisher, after the disaster, declared that the
'performance' in the auditorium was just as carefully organized as that
on the stage. Were these the baying predecessors of the audience at La
Scala who would so viciously boo Pavarotti for a fluffed top-note in
Verdi's *Don Carlo* in the 1990s?

Today there remains no single precisely identified explanation for
the initial failure of so popular a work. No doubt it was caused by a
combination of factors. Reasons for the initial flop of Rossini's *Il
barbiere di Siviglia* (supporters of Paisiello's rival opera on the same
subject were in the audience), of Verdi's *La traviata* (the music was
deemed not to suit the voices of the singers), and of Britten's *Gloriana*
(the Royal gala audience found it tedious and offensive) are not hard
to find. Audience crassness – a determination to draw blood as cruelly
as possible – is the only likely explanation of the failure of *Madama
Butterfly*. It is true that the *Corriere della Sera* reported at the time that
'the public that had assembled in the theatre in the assurance of
witnessing a new triumph for its favourite composer passed without
transition from excessive optimism to harsh criticism, condemning
without consideration.' But Puccini, as we know, was not everybody's
favourite composer in Milan, nor did everybody assemble 'in the
assurance of witnessing a new triumph'.

The uproar, in the long run, harmed Puccini no more than the
disastrous première of the much more provocative *The Rite of Spring*
damaged Stravinsky in Paris nine years later. But it wounded him
deeply at the time. Though not all the reviews were hostile, those that
were knew exactly where to strike. One of them struck twice in a
single sentence by calling *Butterfly* 'that diabetic opera, the result of an
automobile accident'.

Revisions, Puccini realized, would have to be made quickly if his
opera was to be recognized as a cut above *Iris*, Mascagni's rival
Japanese confection to a libretto by Illica, which had already been
presented in Rome, Milan, New York and Philadelphia. So, in the
interests of brevity, he pared away some of the character sketches of
Butterfly's friends and relatives in Act I, in the correct belief that they
merely delayed the arrival of the big love duet. He inserted an interval
between the two parts of the long second act, thus making the work
technically a three-àct opera (but thereby lengthening its running time
again). And he awarded Pinkerton – who had been out of the action

from the end of Act I – a proper aria, the distraught 'Addio, fiorito asil' ('Farewell, flowery refuge') in the final scene, when he withdraws from the house, belatedly aware of his cruelty and unable to face the wife he deserted. Though this aria (short as it is) could have seemed gratuitous – and the composer's opponents were quick to point out the fact – it is absolutely essential in operatic terms.

These and other changes in the end helped to do the trick. When the revamped *Madama Butterfly* was presented three months later at the provincial but welcoming Teatro Grande, Brescia, between Milan and Verona, it was as great a success as the earlier version had been a failure. True, there was a thrilling new exponent of the title role, the beautiful Ukrainian dramatic soprano, Salomea Krusceniski, who had already appeared as Manon in Cremona and would later become a sensational Salome under Toscanini at La Scala. Perhaps her presence helped to turn the work's fortunes – Puccini later admitted that Storchio may have been too doll-like for the role. Butterfly, after all, is a young woman of considerable personality, spirit and determination, who abandons her family and national traditions, accepts the curses of her uncle, and later rejects the advances of a rich Japanese suitor, in order to marry and stay married to the American sailor in whom she totally believes. But as the other principal singers, and the conductor were the same as in Milan, it does seem that *Madama Butterfly* owed its new success to the composer's meticulous revisions and, perhaps above all, to the presence of a more open-minded audience, even in a town only fifty miles from Milan. Rather further away – in the ever-friendly Teatro Colón in Buenos Aires, under the baton of Toscanini in July 1904 – it was again a hit.

Yet the structure of the piece continued to disturb Puccini. Even today, with a less than compelling cast and a half-hearted conductor, the love scene that forms the climax of Act I can seem to sprawl. And Act II – which the composer called 'eternal' and Giacosa called 'interminable' – all too easily becomes unrewardingly long if the conductor fails to pace it properly. But that could be true of an ineffectual performance of any opera. With its ebb and flow properly caught, the love scene from *Madama Butterfly* is the most perfectly structured, atmospheric, and truthful of all Puccini's love scenes.

But after the Milan débâcle, and even after the Brescia success, the composer and his collaborators remained acutely sensitive to the

Opposite, the Théâtre de l'Opéra-Comique in Paris, where Madama Butterfly had its first French perform-ance in 1906 with Marguérite Carré in the title role. Puccini's revision of the opera softened certain aspects of the story to suit the Opéra-Comique's family audience.

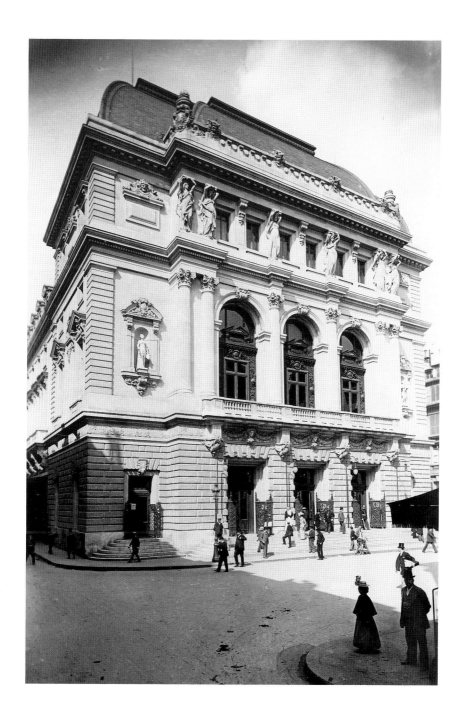

A scene from Scottish Opera's 1987 production of *Madama Butterfly*, which the designer Ezio Frigerio set in an impoverished tenement building. In the scene are Seppo Ruohonen as Lieutenant Pinkerton, Norman Bailey as Sharpless and Anne-Marie Owens as Suzuki.

possibility that *Madama Butterfly* might contain too much music and too many words. Mozart, after the première of *Die Entführung aus dem Serail*, was able to resist the put-down ('too many notes my dear Mozart') he received from his royal patron, but Puccini lacked his predecessor's sublime self-confidence. So when the opportunity came to present *Madama Butterfly* at Covent Garden the following year, he responded with further cuts, as he also did for the first American performances, sung by a travelling company in English translation.

Not even these satisfied him, however, and by the time of the French première at the Paris Opéra-Comique in 1906 he was still making cuts and alterations. By then Act I had lost about thirty pages, and the two linked parts of the original Act II had become a separate Act II and III, much against Puccini's instincts. It was, after all, the linking passage in Belasco's play – Butterfly's silent vigil which, performed by Blanche Bates, had held the audience enthralled for ten minutes – which had first attracted Puccini to the idea of a *Butterfly* opera. From the start, he had wanted Act II to be performed in a single sweep, thereby 'reaching the end having held the public nailed to their seats for an hour and a half'. To which he added: 'Monstrous, but the life of the opera depends on it.'

Did he eventually cut and change too much? As evidence of his indecision, there were now four different versions of *Madama Butterfly* to choose from. Instead of having a clear-cut *ur*-text, future generations of conductor and director would have to try to decide – if, at any rate, they were dedicated enough to differentiate between one version and another – what Puccini actually wanted. But then, since Puccini himself never really knew what he wanted, the text of *Madama Butterfly*, like the different versions of Bizet's *Carmen* and the running order of Jacques Offenbach's *Les Contes d'Hoffmann*, will always be controversial.

Puristic conductors – or at least those who, almost as a matter of principle, believe that a composer's 'first version' of an opera is likely to be superior to his final one – increasingly lean towards an uncut (or almost uncut) *Butterfly*. Others, in the interests of 'seeing how it goes', like to restore a little of the material Puccini so ruthlessly hacked away. Still others are content to treat the Paris version as the most authentic, recognizing it to be musically the tightest, even if the necessity for two intervals breaks the work's continuity and ekes out the evening. It is generally agreed that the best solution is to make all or most of the Puccini-approved cuts, but to retain his original two-act format, and sometimes to restore passages usually omitted, if or when the occasion demands it. This, inevitably, puts a strain on the principal singer, who – once she has appeared for the wedding scene – is hardly off the stage for the rest of the performance. But dramatic compensation is provided in these circumstances by the greater emotional thrust.

The success of the Paris version, however, was achieved at a price. Albert Carré, director of the Opéra-Comique, wanted an opera to suit his bourgeois audience, who ritualistically attended performances on Sunday afternoons after a brasserie lunch on the nearby Grands Boulevards. *Butterfly*, like *Carmen*, had to comply with their tastes. Moreover Madame Carré, whom Puccini nicknamed 'Mme Pomme de Terre' ('Mrs Potato'), had been allotted the title role. The selfishly abrasive, racist side of Pinkerton's character, Carré insisted, must be softened. Not in front of a Paris audience would Pinkerton be allowed to address the servants as 'Mugs One, Two, and Three'; nor, any longer, would he be permitted to order them to serve portions of spiders, flies, and other 'Japanese' delicacies. Even Butterfly's role was to be sentimentalized, to suit 'Mme Pomme de Terre' and her admirers. The result, according to Julian Smith, editor of Ricordi's latest edition of the opera, 'successfully diluted' what Puccini originally intended, transforming a 'daring opera, unconventional in its structure, and unsparing in its delivery of what for its time was an unusually pointed moral and social message' into something 'perilously close to sentimental melodrama'.

Yet in spite of all its problems, and in spite of Smith's doubts, *Madama Butterfly* even in its Paris version is Puccini's greatest opera. In it he achieved a beauty, subtlety, and intensity of utterance he never surpassed. *Bohème* was more perfect, *Tosca* more powerful, and his later works more sophisticated, but *Butterfly* was the lynchpin of his entire output, and his long struggles with it suggest that he was aware of the fact. It formed the summit of his melodious 'middle period', which had begun eleven years earlier with *Manon Lescaut*. It marked the end of a strongly personal and lyrical line of works, and he knew it. Thereafter, ever more keenly attuned to what was happening elsewhere in Europe, he would strike out in new directions, continuing to develop the richness of his musical language.

Even in its shorter Paris version, *Butterfly* is the longest of his operas. In spite of his problems with its structure, the nature of its story and its leisurely but by no means undramatic musical unfurling, serve to justify a time-span as great as Verdi's *Aida*, and lengthier than the same composer's *Otello* or *Falstaff*. Yet he knew this was required by all his musical ideas for it. His infiltration into it of Japanese tunes, pentatonic scales, and the tinkle of little bells has been dismissed as naïve – music of the 'Postcard from Nagasaki' variety. But it is done with such beautiful discretion, and it merges so effortlessly with Puccini's own Italianism, that the effect is invariably touching, shedding Puccini's own special light on Butterfly's vulnerable personality. To call it kitsch would be to miss its point. To suggest that it will outlive the refined but inert music of Toro Takemitsu – Puccini's Japanese obverse and today's most celebrated linksman between the music of East and West – may seem rude, but it is a point worth making on Puccini's behalf.

4

Emmy Destinn, at the age of thirty-three, as Minnie in *La fanciulla del West*. This portrait of the great Czech soprano appeared in the *Illustrated London News* in tribute to her Covent Garden appearance in the role in June 1911.

My life is a sea of sadness, and I am stuck with it.

Giacomo Puccini,
after his motoring accident

Beyond Butterfly 1904–10

The abused and vulnerable Cio-Cio-San – 'Madama Butterfly' – was
Puccini's perfect heroine. But the Bible-punching, gun-toting Minnie
– 'The Girl of the Golden West' – was someone for whom he had
feelings, too. Recognizing her to be the subject of his next opera
nevertheless took him even longer than usual. There were rival claims
to be considered. The medieval Santa Margherita di Cortona and the
Hunchback of Notre Dame sought his attention. So did the eternally
tempting Marie Antoinette, whom Puccini, in a letter to Illica,
described as 'a soul in torment – first act, prison; second act – the
trial; third act – the execution'. As he put it enthusiastically: 'Three
short acts, stirring enough to take one's breath away.'

But a triptych of tales by Gogol, built around the oversized
operatic personality of Fyodor Chaliapin, also looked promising,
as did the decadent and claustrophobic world of Oscar Wilde's
play, *A Florentine Tragedy*. The triptych idea soon came to nothing,
though it probably planted the seeds of *Il trittico*, the rather
different trio of one-act operas Puccini eventually wrote. *A Florentine
Tragedy*, on the other hand, could have been a rival for Strauss's
similarly claustrophobic *Salome*, unveiled in Germany in 1905.
Giulio Ricordi, however, failed to recognize the former's
possibilities. He thought the play 'stupid' – which it certainly was
not – and the work was eventually composed (rather well, as has
been belatedly recognized) by Alexander Zemlinsky, Schoenberg's
teacher, in 1916.

Puccini's painful indecision was understandable. Remembering the
initial débâcle of *Madama Butterfly*, and the taunts that were hurled at
him, he did not want to go through the same humiliating experience
again, in Milan or anywhere else. He wanted his next choice of subject
to be really foolproof, and – so much for the theory that Puccini liked
to take the easy way out – he wanted it to break new musical ground.
In 1904, in the wake of *Madama Butterfly*, he had disclosed his
disheartenment to Illica: 'I find it impossible that I should have to

scribble more notes. And anyway, people are sick now of my sugary music.'

So once again he went round in circles, contemplating this and rejecting that, then reconsidering his rejections, before finally settling for what today may seem the obvious – though it must have seemed quite improbable at the time. The work he next composed was an operatic precursor of the spaghetti western, based on another play by David Belasco, author of the play upon which *Madama Butterfly* was based. Whatever his initial fears about working with Belasco again, he managed to conquer them. Such an opera, he decided, would have a guaranteed success not only in Italy but in America, the land to which his attention was increasingly turning. Why, then, did he take so long to produce it?

Keeping tabs on the international progress of his earlier operas increasingly preoccupied him, but it became an obsession in the case of *Madama Butterfly*. Its long and difficult birth, and its subsequent precarious health, made him particularly attentive to its welfare. On the one hand, he self-critically dismissed it – along with *La bohème* – as an 'old carcass'. On the other, he could not let go of it. In the summer of 1905 he pursued it to South America, where it was staged to high acclaim at a starry Puccini festival in Buenos Aires, along with the early *Edgar* (which, for the occasion, he revised for the third time)

Puccini en route to Buenos Aires, where *Madama Butterfly* was staged to great acclaim at a festival in 1905

and three other works. This was his first Atlantic crossing, thanks to
an invitation extended to him and Elvira by the Argentine newspaper,
La Prensa. Then, in the autumn, he caught up on its first London
production (which had opened while he was in Buenos Aires) and
developed his friendship with Sybil Seligman, a thirty-seven-year-old
opera-lover whom he had met previously at the London home of
Paolo Tosti, music tutor to the British royal family and composer of a
famous 'Farewell'.

Of all Puccini's extra-marital relationships, this was one of the few
in which the name of the woman is known. The explanation is
simple. It was the one that endured the longest and that mattered the
most, perhaps particularly after the powerful love they had for each
other had gradually given way to friendship. The wife of a London
banker, she was a talented amateur singer and woman of culture, who
travelled in Italy and (happily for Puccini) spoke good Italian. Though
an air of mystery hung over their friendship, the most thorough of
Puccini's biographers, Mosco Carner, has confirmed that it 'began as a
passionate love affair' and became 'one of the few genuine friendships
which Puccini was able to form'. The composer confided in her, wrote
to her frequently, and received from her the kind of artistic
nourishment he was denied by the jealous Elvira.

Extravagantly, Puccini called her his 'Sybil of Cumae' (the most
famous of Greek-Italian oracles, who guided Aeneas through the
Underworld) and said she was the person who came nearest to
understanding his nature. She was to outlive him by eleven years, and
her son, Vincent Seligman, later chronicled their friendship in his
book, *Puccini Among Friends*. It was Sybil Seligman who suggested
basing an opera on Oscar Wilde's *A Florentine Tragedy*, which Puccini
– until Ricordi put him off it – deemed a 'beautiful, inspired, strong,
and tragic' subject. The plight of Wilde's Bianca (compared with
Strauss's Salome), torn between her husband and her lover, would
make a work 'more human, more real, and nearer the feelings of the
man in the street' – and closer, he might have added, to his own heart.
A little later he would find such a character in *Il tabarro*, the first of
the three one-act operas forming *Il trittico*.

Sybil Seligman was clearly in tune with Puccini's musical
personality. Among her suggestions to him was an opera based on
Tolstoy's *Anna Karenina*, a subject he backed away from, although it

Puccini's affair with Sybil Seligman, a talented amateur singer and wife of a London banker, began passionately and ended as a deep and enduring friendship. Puccini received from her the artistic nourishment he was denied by Elvira.

might have suited him to perfection (it would later daunt Benjamin Britten, a composer who could have brought a similar lyricism to the subject but who likewise had second thoughts about it). Finally, after toying with Pierre Louÿs's *La Femme et la Pantin* ('The Woman and the Puppet'), a sado-masochistic novel filled with foretastes of *Turandot*, Puccini at last hit upon David Belasco's *The Girl of the Golden West*.

Could his partnership with the popular playwright work a second time? Having reached desperation point in his search for a subject, he made an effort to see three Belasco plays during his visit to New York in 1907 for the American première of *Madama Butterfly*. He was in a nervous state. Elvira was with him, but he consoled himself by buying a new speed boat with the money he received from a rich autograph

This caricature by Caruso, drawn during rehearsals at the New York Metropolitan in 1907, shows Caruso himself as Pinkerton, Antonio Scotti as Sharpless, Angelo Bada as Goro and Geraldine Farrar as Butterfly.

hunter for jotting down the opening notes of Musetta's Waltz Song from *La bohème*. The boat was dispatched to Torre del Lago, where Puccini in due course raced it on the lake and along the Burlamacca Canal near the resort of Viareggio.

The cast for the opera displeased him. In a letter to Sybil Seligman he complained that 'the woman' – Geraldine Farrar, who later sang the title-role in the première of *Suor Angelica* – 'was not what she ought to have been' (she for her part called him a 'high irritant' at rehearsals). Nor did he join in the general acclaim for Enrico Caruso, who was singing not only Pinkerton but leading roles in three other Puccini operas. He admitted to Caruso's voice being magnificent, but commented that laziness and arrogance prevented him from learning anything.

Declaring that he had seen as much as he wanted of America, Puccini returned to Europe with Belasco's Wild West melodrama very much on his mind. In Italy it had already been strongly recommended to him by his close friend, the Marchesi Piero Antinori, a member of the celebrated Tuscan wine-making family whose name continues to adorn many of Italy's best bottles (indeed the present Marchesi Piero, twenty-fifth generation holder of the title, has helped to revolutionize

Puccini playing one of his favourite roles: that of the captain of his motor boat *Butterfly* on the lake at Torre del Lago

the Italian wine industry). Now he sought the advice of Sybil Seligman, who was so enthusiastic that she had an Italian translation of the play made for him and dispatched to Torre del Lago.

Until then Puccini had prevaricated. Although the play had been written for Belasco's original Butterfly, Blanche Bates – hailed as 'America's Sarah Bernhardt' – Puccini was not yet quite convinced that it would be a suitable vehicle for one of his own star sopranos; and although he was again seduced by Belasco's atmospheric effects, including Californian minstrels, panoramic views, and a blizzard scene incorporating wind and snow machines, he thought the play itself a 'hotchpotch'. It was Sybil Seligman's powerful belief in it that tipped the balance in its favour. To get him moving, she offered to help him track down some original Red Indian songs and other background material.

As usual, however, there were libretto problems. On Puccini's behalf, Illica was already fully occupied with work on *The Austrian Woman*, or *Maria Antonietta*, Puccini's provisional titles for the Marie Antoinette opera he was still hoping to compose. Moreover, Giacosa having just died, a new poetic talent had to be found urgently. One Ricordi recommendation was Carlo Zangarini, a young Bolognese poet, writer and journalist who had what seemed to Puccini the advantage of an American mother and therefore a grasp of the English language. The trouble was that Zangarini was over-ambitious, wanting to fill not only Illica's role as librettist but Giacosa's as well, whereas Puccini wanted Guelfo Civinini, a fellow Tuscan, to deal with the poetic side of the text.

So once again the composer found himself grappling with a collaborator who refused to accept that Puccini's word was law. The ensuing disagreement grew so fraught that it finally had to be resolved by litigation. Puccini, predictably, won his way, but the process caused equally predictable delays, and transformed Zangarini from someone the composer initially admired into someone he was almost unable to work with. In truth, neither Zangarini nor Civinini was a patch on Illica or Giacosa, whose opinions (in spite of their battles) Puccini valued and whose appeasement he had generally found to be worth the effort. But *La fanciulla del West* survived its early vicissitudes all the same, and became what Puccini wanted it to be: an escape route, as he self-torturingly saw it, from his own 'sugary' music.

But not quite yet. To Giulio Ricordi, he confided that 'this *Girl* is a tremendously difficult work'. He was unhappy with the ending of Belasco's play, and was determined to change it. He had further productions of his previous works to inspect. One of them, the Viennese première of *Madama Butterfly* in the autumn of 1907, represented a sort of revenge on Gustav Mahler, who continued to detest Puccini's music from the *Bohème* period onwards but whose reign over the Vienna Opera was now in jeopardy. With Elvira, Puccini visited Egypt early in 1908, primarily for yet another production of *Madama Butterfly* but also to see the sights that had inspired *Aida.* By the autumn he was still restless, complaining of a serious throat infection (the first hint perhaps of what was to befall him sixteen years later), drifting from one soporific Tuscan summer retreat to another, and bemoaning their shortfalls by letter to Sybil Seligman. Unlike Mozart, he was not a composer who could produce masterpieces while on the move from one place to another. He needed the right conditions, and was too easily deflected by the wrong ones.

Puccini visited Egypt in 1908 with Elvira to explore the inspiration behind *Aida*. Unsurprisingly, his car stood in readiness while he sampled the experience of riding a camel.

Puccini seized every possible distraction from composition around this time, even in the inspirational surroundings of Torre del Lago, the thought of which, while he was in America, had made him express his deep longing for his 'perfumed woods', for 'the wind that blows my way from the sea', for 'the beautiful shape of the poplar and the pine tree, the branches hanging over the shady roads'. Puccini was a poet who claimed to loathe 'the train, top hats, evening clothes', even if his detractors dismissed him as an opportunistic musical businessman.

At Torre del Lago, he declared, he was able to live like 'a modern Druid' with his temple, his house and his study. He reported to Sybil Seligman that he was at last getting down to work again. Yet over this delightful landscape in the autumn of 1908 there loomed a drama so violent and sudden that it would affect him for the rest of his life, and the name of the person at the centre of it would be carved deep into his soul. The name – Doria Manfredi – could have been that of one of Puccini's sad, victimized operatic heroines, as people were quick to point out when the details of her tragedy became public knowledge.

She was, in fact, a local villager – prototype, as people sagely remarked later, of the slave girl Liù in *Turandot* – who had been brought up in a hovel near the lake and had worked from the age of sixteen as a maid at the plush Villa Puccini. Elvira was a notoriously difficult employer, eager to hire and fire, but Doria appears to have been patient and dutiful. Her very quietness, however, went against her. Having helped to nurse Puccini on his long, slow journey back to health after his car accident, and being attentive to his every whim, she gradually aroused Elvira's easily-roused suspicions.

Every doubt Elvira had ever had about her husband's fidelity – and which had prompted her to booby-trap his trouser pockets with camphor and his drinks with bromides – now burst violently into the open. Doria was publicly denounced. She was the root of all that was wrong with the Puccini marriage. She was her husband's 'slut', details of whose immorality Elvira began spreading round the village. Suspicion turned into obsession. The simple villagers, not without reason, became convinced that Elvira possessed the evil eye. Once – in the manner of Act IV of Mozart's *Le nozze di Figaro* – Puccini found his wife in the garden at night, disguised in one of his own suits, hoping to encounter Doria in the darkness. Though the girl by now had been sacked, Elvira's harassment of her continued. As Puccini

The unfortunate Doria
Manfredi, who committed
suicide after Elvira accused
her of having an affair
with Puccini

miserably reported to Sybil, Elvira had got to the stage of screaming
insults at Doria and her relatives in the street, complaining to the local
priest, and demanding that the guilty girl be driven from the village.

In the end, the wretched Doria chose a different way out. In
January 1909 she poisoned herself in her parents' house, and lay in
agony for several days before she died. The autopsy showed her to
have been a virgin. Her family, seeking revenge, demanded legal
action and were not – or at any rate not immediately – appeased by
Puccini's offer of a bribe. Elvira was arrested, brought to court in Pisa,
found guilty and sentenced to seven months in prison. An appeal was
lodged. A bigger bribe was offered and this time the family accepted.
But the humiliation Puccini suffered on his wife's behalf took its toll.
They agreed upon a trial separation. Their son, by then twenty-three,
threatened to leave for Africa. Puccini declared his life to be
'irretrievably ruined'. The Italian press, relishing the story, called it a
wonderful subject for an opera.

By then *La fanciulla del West* had almost ceased to be a subject. For
eight months, Puccini had hardly written a note. Yet when he finally
activated himself, he worked with fierce intensity. During his summer

sojourn at Torre del Lago in 1910 he reported to Giulio Ricordi that he had completed his opera, orchestration and all, which left the way clear for its première in New York in the December of that year.

It was inevitable that the music of the opera, when finally performed, was said by some to show signs of dwindling inspiration. As one critic put it, the tragedy of Doria had left its 'corrosive mark' on *La fanciulla del West*. 'Failing inspiration', however, was something of which Puccini had already been accused more than once, and would be again. The point about *La fanciulla* was that it was different from anything he had written before. He had, in fact, achieved exactly what he had set out to do – which was to escape from what he called the sugary world of *Madama Butterfly* and to chart new territory – but people, as usual, were unwilling either to recognize this or to forgive him for it.

Although his reconciliation with Elvira took time, it was something which, in the end, both of them wanted – if only, perhaps, because there seemed no real alternative. Plainly, their son Tonio preferred the status quo, however dreadful it seemed for much of the time. Puccini himself, after a spell in the company of his old friend, Ciccio Tosti, in Rome, accepted his responsibilities with new gravity. He had denied from the beginning that he had been involved in any way with Doria Manfredi. Yet there is no doubt that a closeness of some sort existed. Not all love affairs, after all, are consummated. Puccini was a vulnerable and increasingly lonely man, and Doria was a recognizable embodiment of several of his heroines, both past and future.

About Doria's total innocence, we shall never be quite sure. Not everything Elvira said about her may have been wrong. Did she have ideas 'above her station'? Did she hero-worship Puccini? Did he encourage her? Elvira claimed that she had shown suicidal tendencies long before she killed herself, and that she possessed a hysterical streak. But who knows what life with the Puccinis must have been like for a simple peasant girl, or how – even before accusations began to be hurled at her – she reacted to Elvira's constant bullying? Puccini himself, in sympathizing with her predicament, may merely have made matters worse for them all, but he paid the penalty for it for the rest of his life.

Whether or not aspects of the tragedy materialized later in *Suor Angelica* or *Turandot*, as some commentators have suggested, is impossible to say. The private lives of composers do not necessarily have a bearing on their compositions, or at any rate not necessarily in so obvious a way, as the music of Mozart and Beethoven makes abundantly plain. The ill-fated Sister Angelica and the slave girl Liù, the two last of Puccini's 'vulnerable little women', may conceivably have been modelled on Doria Manfredi. He certainly confessed that he wept with 'nostalgia, tenderness, and pain' at the thought of them, though that was something he had also done over their operatic predecessors.

Similarly the icy Princess in each opera – and it is significant, perhaps, that Turandot and the Principessa in *Suor Angelica* each held the same imperious rank – may have been modelled on Elvira, or even on his own mother. Yet they are all typical Puccinian personalities, well within his range as an opera composer. What can be asserted more confidently is that there was no trace of any of them to be found in *La fanciulla del West*, perhaps because that work was Puccini's

David Belasco (left), the American playwright, solemnly sealing his friendship with Toscanini, (centre) and Puccini at the time of the première of *La fanciulla del West* at the New York Metropolitan.

escape route from what was happening to him at the time, but perhaps also because his mind simply did not operate that way.

Indeed, the Manfredi episode coincided with a strengthening of his resolve to make *La fanciulla del West* a different sort of Puccini opera, from which all elements of sweetness would be ruthlessly expunged. It would also – unusually for Puccini – have a happy ending and a heroine who, far from being a 'victim', knew exactly how to exert a kindly control over the men around her. In addition, it would invade Wagnerian territory by embracing the possibility of human redemption, even if Minnie's final appearance on horseback was hardly as apocalyptic as Brünnhilde's in *Götterdämmerung*.

Wagner's influence on aspects of his music was something Puccini never concealed. It had already been audible in *Manon Lescaut*, and in his own system of leitmotif, which he employed so productively in *Madama Butterfly*. It was not in vain that he journeyed to Bayreuth in 1912 to experience the religious fervour of *Parsifal*, his favourite Wagner opera, in its proper surroundings – although, being the man he was, he also did it to escape from Elvira in company with his latest conquest, a young German aristocrat, the Baroness Josephine von Stängel.

Booking into their Bayreuth hotel, Puccini concealed himself behind the pseudonym of Archimede Rossi, which prevented him, to his sorrow, from being introduced formally to Wagner's widow, Cosima. It must also have greatly disappointed Josephine, who was not content to have a secret lover. Her aim, quite outspokenly, was to oust Elvira and live with Puccini in the seaside resort of Viareggio, where she had first met him in 1911, soon after the moderately successful Italian première of *La fanciulla del West* in Rome.

But by then, in America, the work had become one of the triumphs of Puccini's life. It was the first world première to take place at the New York Metropolitan since the opera house's opening in 1883, and Puccini, who had been invited to attend the preparations, was feted from the moment he arrived on the liner *George Washington* a month before the first night. He had sailed across the Atlantic in style, in the ship's most lavish suite, with every expense paid by the opera company. His son Tonio was with him, but Elvira had been persuaded, as a by-product of their 'reconciliation', to remain in Italy – a demand that hurt her deeply and made her feel, as she put it,

'nothing but a pygmy'. The playwright David Belasco was among the
crowd waiting to greet Puccini at the dock. Toscanini, who was to
conduct the première, had already telegraphed him with reassuring
news about the rehearsals. The Czech soprano Emmy Destinn
(already one of the world's favourite Cio-Cio-Sans) and Enrico
Caruso, in the leading roles, were soon to be hailed by Puccini as his
'passionate and precious collaborators'.

As the opening night approached, America made it plain that
Puccini was the man of the moment. In spite of thorough precautions,
black-market tickets for the performance were fetching thirty times
the official price. Even the ever-doubtful composer came to believe he
had a success on his hands. He wrote to Elvira that he was content
with his work, and that Toscanini was 'the zenith – kind, good,
adorable'. The production, overseen by Giulio Ricordi's son Tito, did
him proud, with splendid scenery and eight horses in Act III, just as
he had hoped. Outside, the New York streets were jammed. Inside,
there were more than fifty curtain calls, most of them for Puccini
himself. To a delighted Sybil Seligman he wrote euphorically that *La
fanciulla del West* was his best opera. It proved, he said, that he had
not 'dried up' and that he was still capable of 'moving forward'.

Move forward he undoubtedly did, even if not everybody was
aware of it. Though the public adored *La fanciulla del West* as a show,
and revelled in the quiet emotion and almost cinematic 'slow fade' of
the final 'Addio mia California' – which drifts atmospherically into
silence via the sound of high string tone, the gleam of a celesta, and
the softest stroke of a bass drum – a lack of melodic interest was
detected. Where were the arias? Where were the tunes? What had
similarly been said about Verdi's *Falstaff* – and what is still said about
it by those who prefer the memorably clear-cut melodies of *La
traviata* and *Il trovatore* – was repeated about *La fanciulla del West*.
The trouble with arias that do not have a conventional beginning and
end, and are thus semi-concealed within the flow of the music, is that
inexperienced or unwilling listeners often fail to recognize them as
arias at all. To claim that such an opera is 'all melody' is, for this sort
of listener, sure proof that it is nothing of the kind. Had the composer
of 'E lucevan le stelle', people asked, lost his touch?

In fact, *La fanciulla del West* contained plenty of melodies, plenty
of harmonic and instrumental innovations, and plenty of action, but

the way they were packaged was not to everybody's taste. Puccini had wanted to prove that his genius was not dependent on the presence of another 'Che gelida manina', and he had succeeded. Maurice Ravel perceptively recognized that here was a work in which Puccini had put the orchestra in the role of the protagonist. Moreover, by building up the minor scene of Minnie's Bible reading to the tough gold miners into an element of considerable importance, Puccini could be said to have intervened in the natural progress of the story with a decisiveness that made its mark on the whole opera.

The Bible reading, indeed, turned out to be one of the features of *La fanciulla del West* that made it 'different' from Puccini's other works. It was not as elaborate as Gurnemanz's address to the knights in Wagner's *Parsifal,* yet it did convey a morality that the German composer would have understood, and it did help to make sense out of a denouement in which Minnie persuades the vengeful miners not to lynch Dick Johnson, her outlaw lover. Without this final act of salvation, *La fanciulla del West* might have become a sort of '*Tosca del West*', with Johnson hanged and Minnie killed while trying to rescue him. The fact that Puccini resisted the temptation shows that he did indeed have a desire to progress into a different sort of opera.

The launching of *La fanciulla del West* in New York in December 1910 was a triumph, however much some of the critics – particularly Italian ones – disliked it for not being another *Tosca* or *Bohème.* Puccini expressed his gratitude to Toscanini by buying him a silver candelabrum at Tiffany's. The nine New York performances led to others in Chicago, Philadelphia, Boston and Baltimore. The composer, returning to Elvira on board the *Lusitania,* wrote of his 'envy' for the Toscaninis, with their 'close family'. When he reached Torre del Lago, his mood remained unchanged. From 'the silence of the village', he informed Toscanini that his happy memories of *La fanciulla del West* were tinged with sorrow – 'those beautiful moments are too few, and they pass too quickly.'

Through disclosures such as these, we realize that Puccini's hard-nosed image was not always what it seemed. As a composer, he has been dismissed as too 'theatrical', and accused of manipulating the emotions of his audience in a way that greater men, such as Verdi, would never do. Yet most composers, including Verdi, do this to some extent – and it would be hard to know where precisely to draw the line between conscious and unconscious manipulation, and hard to decide how much it matters.

To single out this side of Puccini, in order to condemn him for it, is surely humbug. To listen to *La fanciulla del West* with unprejudiced ears is once again to recognize something else: that Puccini was a poet, and nowhere more so than when, in Act I, Minnie and her bandit-on-the-run dance in the saloon to the strains of a little diatonic waltz-tune of the sort that only Puccini could have written and coloured in that particular delicate way. Even the tunes in *La fanciulla del West* that are not Puccini's own are somehow transformed into what sounds like pure Puccini by the way he treats them. It was a knack he had already employed creatively in *Madama Butterfly*, and the nostalgic use of the folk-song, 'The Old Dog Tray', at various points in *La fanciulla del West* shows that he had definitely not lost his touch.

With only one – albeit vitally important – female role, *La fanciulla del West* is based more than any other Puccini opera on the sound of male voices, either solo or in chorus. Not until Britten's *Billy Budd* would a male cast again be employed to such striking effect, and in a not dissimilar manner. Both here and subsequently in *Il trittico*, Puccini began to create atmosphere in new ways. He had seen Debussy's *Pelléas et Mélisande* in Paris in 1906, four years after its première, and he reckoned it to be superior to anything by Richard Strauss because its orchestration, he said, made dissonances sound agreeable, even if its colouring was as unrelieved as 'a Franciscan habit'. It is certainly Debussy, rather than Strauss, whose sound-world is sometimes evoked by *La fanciulla del West*, and by at least two of the three *Trittico* operas. If Puccini's use of the whole-tone scale was borrowed from Debussy, it was an undeniably brilliant borrowing, employed to real purpose. Far from simply superimposing it on his music, he integrated it into his style with unerring flair.

But the first two decades of the twentieth century were in every way a period of enormous musical change, to which a composer of Puccini's perception could hardly fail to react. His responsiveness to Stravinsky – whose *Rite of Spring* he conceded to be 'not without a certain talent' – is audible in *Il tabarro*, the first of the *Trittico* operas, and also later in *Turandot*. In Vienna, he attended the première of Schoenberg's *Gurrelieder*, but stating it to be too dependent on Wagner, he walked out halfway through the performance. Yet he

Puccini returning from New York on the Lusitania after the successful première of *La fanciulla del West* at the Metropolitan. With him is Tito Ricordi, who – to Puccini's displeasure – became head of the great Italian publishing house after his father's death in 1912.

recognized that there was undoubtedly something there – as many
another composer would not have done – and in the year of his death
he took the trouble to go to Florence to hear *Pierrot Lunaire* in a
performance supervised by Schoenberg himself.

No major work of the period, however, was more widely performed
than *La fanciulla del West.* Although it was the most elaborate of all
Puccini's operas to stage, and its orchestral parts were his most
challenging to date, it was nevertheless presented in London, Paris,
Berlin, Vienna, Budapest, Monte Carlo and Milan within a year or so
of its initial chain of American performances. A production in
Liverpool, employing a reduced version of the score, was attended by
the composer in person. Even loyal Brescia, where *Madama Butterfly*
had made its first hit, managed to mount a production of it –
although Puccini, seemingly forgetful of what that very ordinary
North Italian town had done on *Butterfly's* behalf, grumbled about
performing *La fanciulla del West* 'in the provinces', with an orchestra,
as he put it, full of 'dogs'.

The Monte Carlo production, on the other hand, was particularly
splendid, with the young Giovanni Martinelli (who would eventually
replace Caruso as Italy's star tenor) as Dick Johnson. This became, it
was said, Martinelli's 'passport role' to the world's great opera houses,
although it was Caruso who sang it in Paris in 1912.

Whatever its opponents have said against it, *La fanciulla del West*
marked a new start in Puccini's career. It enabled him to burst the
bonds of what he had come to regard as the straitjacket of the
Madama Butterfly sort of opera, and move from a predominantly
feminine world into a more assertively masculine one, but remain
recognizably himself. True, its general suppression of the old-style
Puccini aria meant that the public would never adore it in quite the
same way as *La bohème, Tosca* or *Madama Butterfly.* Yet his decision to
give Johnson a tiny unobtrusive aria towards the end of the last act
showed that he had lost none of his old touch and sense of timing.

In this eloquent two-stanza lament, the outlaw-hero beseeches the
lynch mob to inform Minnie that he has made his escape from the
hanging tree. In reply, cutting across what could have become a third
stanza, the malevolent Sheriff Rance – the Californian equivalent of
Scarpia in *Tosca* – punches him on the face. Because it comes so late in
the opera, the aria is all the more potent in its effect. It is music more

succinct, and more subtle, than Cavaradossi's comparable 'E lucevan le stelle' in *Tosca*. It also, like the rest of *La fanciulla*, requires its listeners to use their ears.

Puccini himself believed that in order to know *La fanciulla del West*, two or three hearings were necessary. Because it lacks the instant appeal of its popular predecessors, it does not hold so prominent a place in the repertoire. But as a result, every production of it is an event and, if the performance is a good one, it enables you to marvel at the opera anew. Happily, it has had many fine performances in its time, and has attracted some of the finest dramatic singers of the century. Puccini was right to feel pleased with it.

5

The Casino and its terrace
at Monte Carlo, where *La
rondine*, Puccini's politically
controversial comedy, had
its delayed première in
March 1917

People are sick now of my sugary music.

Giacomo Puccini, between the
composition of *Madama Butterfly* and
La fanciulla del West

Puccini's Wars 1910–17

But what then? Once again the old search for a subject began. Since Puccini knew that the selection and composition of an opera could occupy him for years, and since he was now into his fifties, he was more than ever aware that he could not afford to make a mistake. Yet his next work was soon to be considered the biggest mistake of his career. Today there are Puccini devotees who know *La rondine*, if at all, only through the soprano's song, 'Chi il bel sogno di Doretta', so ravishingly voiced (along with the more famous 'O mio babbino caro' from *Gianni Schicchi*) by Kiri Te Kanawa in the film of *A Room with a View*. The title of the opera is almost always wrongly pronounced (it is La RON-di-ne, with the accent on the first syllable). And its meaning, 'The Swallow', is a mystery to the uninitiated (it refers to the heroine, who flies from her nest but sadly returns to it at the end).

Very occasional attempts to resuscitate *La rondine* – such as Opera North's plucky and well-intentioned, but crudely misconceived, production in Leeds in 1994 – usually miss its elusive flavour by a considerable distance. But *La rondine*, for all its elusiveness, was not a mistake. It is, in fact, a very special piece, and a by no means wrong-headed invasion of an area of operatic territory Puccini had hitherto avoided – that of gentle tragi-comedy.

The initiative for this improbable addition to the Puccini canon came originally and surprisingly from Austria in the form of a cash offer. At a time when Europe was in turmoil, Italy itself being on the brink of war with its neighbour, such a project provided scope for – at the very least – embarrassment of a sort that a composer more politically astute than Puccini would have instantly recognized. But Puccini, like his contemporary Richard Strauss, was as weak on politics as he was strong on musical escapism.

The thought of serving as a wartime ambulance driver, as Ravel did in France, would never have occurred to him, in spite of his fondness for motor vehicles. Alhough his son, Tonio, did enlist in the Army

A scene from the Opera North production of *La rondine* in Leeds in 1994 – a courageous, if not wholly successful, treatment of a seriously undervalued work

Motor Ambulance division, Puccini was content to entrench himself in Torre del Lago, and even to ignore the not very demanding opportunity to join Debussy, Saint-Saëns, Elgar, Edward German, André Messager, and even Mascagni in contributing to Sir Hall Caine's *King Albert's Book*, a collection of cultural odds and ends which the *Daily Telegraph* published in London in tribute to 'Brave

Little Belgium'. Debussy – who certainly knew where his loyalties lay – admittedly produced nothing more memorable than his *Berceuse heroïque* or 'Heroic Lullaby', but at least it was the right sort of gesture. As he explained: 'It was all I was able to achieve, having been physically affected by the proximity of hostilities, not to mention my own feeling of inferiority in military matters, never having handled a rifle.'

Puccini, at Torre del Lago, had often handled a rifle. As evidence of this, his armoury can be inspected to this day at the Villa Puccini. But to suggest that he should have been prepared to use it on Austrians rather than on wild birds might seem unfair. He was not a hostile man and, as time passed, he was not unaware of what was happening elsewhere in Europe ('whether it be victory or defeat,' he wrote in pacifist terms to Sybil Seligman, 'human lives are sacrificed.'). But his loyalty was mostly to himself and his friends. By 1914 he had friends everywhere, and he considered Austria – at least until war prevented him from going there in 1915 – simply a pleasant place to travel to, via the scenic excitement of the Alps, with the possibility of a performance of one of his (or Richard Strauss's) operas

The hunting room in the villa at Torre del Lago. To the right of Puccini's gun cabinet are pictures of Sybil Seligman and of Puccini with his librettists Giacosa and Illica.

in Vienna at the end of it, plus the prospect of good company and a
few promising flirtations.

The war, therefore, was principally a nuisance that might get in the
way of his travel plans – 'How I long to travel! When will this cursed
war be over?' he asked mournfully. It might also obstruct progress on
his next opera. Certainly *La rondine* was not an idea that came his way
immediately. His options, shortly before the war, had looked even less
than usually promising, numerous though they were. A Spanish
comedy entitled *The Cheerful Soul* competed with a strange and
spectral tragedy by Gerhart Hauptmann; a collaboration with
Gabriele d'Annunzio on the subject of the Children's Crusade; and
Ouida's sentimental tale of the *Two Little Wooden Shoes* (which
attracted Puccini, it seems, simply because Mascagni was also attracted
to it). But these all proved insufficiently enticing in the long-term.
George du Maurier's *Trilby* was more promisingly considered, and
once again Oscar Wilde's *Florentine Tragedy* was contemplated but still
found wanting. 'Is there nothing to be seen in London at the
theatres?' he asked Sybil Seligman plaintively.

On one of his visits to Vienna just before the outbreak of war –
where that city's favourite soprano, the flamboyant Maria Jeritza,
happened to be appearing in what was locally translated as *Das
Mädchen aus dem West* – he struck what looked like gold. Attending
an operetta at the frivolous Karltheater in the autumn of 1913 (it was
bombed into oblivion during World War II), he was taken aside and
invited to compose an operetta of his own. Thanks to the promise of
a fat fee, and to the flattering award of the Star of the Order of Franz
Joseph, the chequered history of what ultimately became *La rondine*
now began. After complications remarkable even by Puccini's
standards, the work was finally staged four years later, not in Vienna,
nor in Italy, but in the compromise surroundings of the Monte
Carlo Opera.

What the Austrians expected of Puccini, and what he eventually
produced, differed considerably. Naturally enough, the directors of the
Karltheater wanted Italy's most illustrious composer to give them a
German operetta intermingling spoken words and music in the
tradition of Johann Strauss and Franz Lehár. Although Puccini loved
Lehár – a picture of whom held the place of honour on top of his
piano at Torre del Lago – this was not quite what he had in mind. As

Opposite, the glamorous
Czech-born soprano Maria
Jeritza, idolized in Vienna –
and by Puccini – for her
portrayals of Tosca and of
Minnie in La fanciulla
del West

he succinctly put it after accepting Vienna's offer of 200,000 kronen along with property rights: 'I will never write an operetta; a comic opera, yes.'

In case this was not quite clear to his Austrian sponsors, he added that it would be something like Richard Strauss's *Der Rosenkavalier*, 'but more diverting and more organic'. Clearly, then, his ambition was to outshine his German rival Strauss, whose *Elektra* he considered 'a horror' and whose *Die Frau ohne Schatten* he would later dismiss as 'logarithms'. But his reference to *Rosenkavalier* was a herring of the rosiest hue, since what he finally provided was nothing like Strauss's opera at all, but instead an elegant gloss on *La traviata* in which, at the end, he permitted his courtesan heroine to remain poignantly but quite definitely alive.

Although he spent much of World War I quietly at work on *La rondine*, the harmlessness of its *Belle Époque* plot – about two pairs of lovers whose interweaving relationships owed something to Johann Strauss's *Die Fledermaus* and, in a restrained sort of way, to his own *La bohème* – failed to rescue him from the barbs and gibes of opponents who deemed him to be not only escaping from reality but actively encouraging the enemy Austrians.

Yet it would be hard to imagine a man like Puccini facing reality by offering his own musical commentary on the state of Europe, as Britten, for example, would later do in his *War Requiem* (1961). He was simply not that sort of composer. War, for Puccini, was something to retreat from as discreetly as possible. Ironically his discretion at times drew attention to itself. The absence of his name from a group letter objecting to the bombardment of Rheims did him no good at all, and his stilted explanation of his inactivity – 'I want to remain inside the shell of my reserve, adhering to the neutrality that our country has imposed' – was considered pusillanimous, not least because in a careless moment he had admitted himself to be a 'Germanophile'.

As a result, he was accused by the fanatical Léon Daudet (editor of *L'Action Française* and son of Alphonse Daudet, the Provençal author of the *Lettres de mon moulin*) of writing not only an 'enemy opera' but one which would be 'treasonable' to stage in war-torn France. Puccini's artful revenge – to donate the profits of a year of performances of *Tosca* in Paris to wounded soldiers – doubtless

seemed mere expedience to Daudet. But, coming from a man who
disliked parting with his money, this was no mean gesture.

Puccini was, however, less willing to part with Baroness Josephine
von Stängel, even though his ongoing relationship with a German
baroness could hardly be considered tactful at so sensitive a period in
European history. Arranging on one occasion to meet her in Lugano –
an easy journey through the Ticino region along the very route
favoured more recently by corrupt Milanese tax avoiders with secret
Swiss bank accounts – he was refused a visa because of his relationship
with 'a German woman'. But maybe, at that embarrassing moment,
the fifty-nine-year-old Giacomo was as afraid of Elvira finding him
out as of explaining to his demanding baroness that their secret tryst
would have to be indefinitely postponed.

Negotiating with potential Austrian librettists, performers,
publishers, translators and backers while Europe was at war proved
no less problematic for him. The unsympathetic Tito Ricordi, who
had inherited the family firm after his father's death in 1912, made
it plain immediately that he was uninterested in acquiring the
Italian rights to what he regarded as Puccini's Austrian folly. The
loss of Giulio Ricordi – 'Signor Giulio', as Puccini called him –
had hit the composer hard. Giuseppe Giacosa was already dead;
now only Puccini and Illica remained as survivors of the great
quartet, whose planning sessions had been such battlegrounds but
had always been beneficially resolved. Giulio Ricordi, although he
was meant to occupy the presidential chair, was never impartial
enough for that task. Instead, as Illica wrote in his obituary of the
publisher, he became 'one of the most obstinate and most vigorous
belligerents', whereas Puccini himself grew so nervous that
afterwards 'he had to run to the manicurist to have his finger-nails
attended to: he had bitten them off, down to the bone'.

Gruelling and time consuming though these sessions were, they
formed part of Puccini's creative impulse. The point about Giulio, as
one Italian critic has remarked, was that he belonged to an artistic
world driven by publishers' enthusiasms and typically nineteenth-
century passions; his death therefore signified the loss of one of the
last vigorous participating witnesses of nineteenth-century Italian
opera, as Puccini had known it in his youth. For the brutally
businesslike Tito Ricordi, on the other hand, a composer was just a

commodity. 'He called it bad Lehár,' Puccini complained to Sybil
Seligman when Tito showed no enthusiasm for *La rondine*. But the
Casa Ricordi's old rival, Edoardo Sonzogno, jumped at the chance of
at last acquiring a Puccini opera, and even came up with the excellent
advice that the most diplomatic place to stage it would be Monte
Carlo, where, it so happened, Sonzogno had connections.

Having rejected the first Austrian libretto for *La rondine*, Puccini
decided that the second one would suit him – though his ignorance of
the German language meant that a great deal of translation, back-
translation, and re-translation would be required before acceptable
German and Italian versions of the work could be assembled. For the
Italian version – the one that obviously mattered to Puccini and the
one through which the opera would eventually be established
internationally – a new name was added to Puccini's array of librettists
and advisers: Giuseppe Adami. Although Illica was still living, his
relationship with the composer had deteriorated after the death of
Giacosa and, particularly, when all his efforts on behalf of a Marie
Antoinette opera had been made for nothing.

By now Puccini had rightly become concerned about what might
befall *La rondine*, 'given the frightful conditions produced by this
horrible war'. But at least he continued to find the story-line inspiring
enough to continue work on it, even if he never quite made up his
mind about the ending – alternative versions of it exist, with different
escape routes for 'the swallow' from her bitter-sweet amorous
predicament. Puccini's shrewdness as an opera composer, if not as a
politician, had by now convinced him that a Viennese première for *La
rondine* would be a bad idea, but legally he had committed himself to
exactly that.

A private meeting in Switzerland with one of his Austrian contacts
enabled him to strike a satisfactory bargain whereby he would retain a
half share of the rights along with – what really mattered – personal
control over the première. And Monte Carlo, in March 1917, rose to
the occasion. Its light-hearted air, even in wartime, suited Puccini's
most light-hearted opera. Yet the performance, when it finally took
place, was strongly cast and far from insubstantial.

The twenty-five-year-old Gilda dalla Rizza, much admired by the
composer, sang the swallow-like heroine, Magda. Her reward was to
be given the title-role in *Suor Angelica* as well as the part of Lauretta,

the winsome exponent of 'O mio babbino caro' ('O my beloved daddy') in *Gianni Schicchi* two years later. The sweet-toned Tito Schipa was the principal tenor, Ruggero, Puccini's innocent equivalent of Verdi's Alfredo, the charming but feckless lover of the glamorous courtesan Violetta in *La traviata*. The audience, to the composer's delight, found the piece 'moving and comic', just as he wanted them to. The critics were happy with the music – which included two hit numbers, some engagingly insouciant waltzes, some neatly integrated choruses, sufficient love interest, and Puccini's most sparkling orchestration – and the decision to give the proceeds of the première to the war wounded was nothing if not shrewd.

Yet in spite of the good omens, *La rondine* subsequently languished. While it is true that Buenos Aires enjoyed it in May 1917, Puccini had always been popular there and his attitude to the war was no great issue. But its token performances in Italy did not endear themselves to those Italian critics who liked to accuse Puccini – even in a work as progressive as *La fanciulla del West* – of being out of tune with the times. Bologna, where it first appeared, was not too hostile, but Milan in October 1917 was once again so vituperative that Puccini – who initially blamed the serious shortcomings of the performance for the work's failure – lost confidence and decided to rewrite it.

The problem, as he correctly surmised, lay in the last act. By that point in the evening, the two hit numbers had already been and gone. The rueful Riviera denouement, despite being savoured in Monte Carlo, no longer seemed quite so apt. And the action, compared with that of *La traviata*, seemed perfunctory. An update from the world of 'hateful crinolines' to that of 'stylized modern dress' was thought advisable, and other 'improvements' were discussed by the composer and librettist.

But in fact, although *La rondine* has never advanced beyond the fringes of the Puccini repertoire, there was little about the work that needed serious change or justified the composer's usual post-première desire to revise and revise again. Whichever ending is chosen by the performing company, it is an elegant, fastidiously fashioned opera that enabled Puccini to exploit a side of his musical personality he was prone to neglect. On paper, the plot moves well. In performance, the music fits it like the softest, most luxurious of Italian gloves. The

A model of the art nouveau
stage for the original
production of *La rondine* at
the Salle Garnier, Monte
Carlo, in 1917

composer was surely not indulging in self-mockery when he called it one of his most 'sincere' compositions.

Like all soufflés, however, it goes flat easily. For so entrancing a score, performances tend to be too heavy and hard-edged, characterization too crudely drawn. Championing *La rondine* sadly often ends in disaster. Happily, Monte Carlo – which championed it from the start and clearly got it right first time – has continued to nurture it via a modern production that has won high acclaim. Other companies have done less well by the piece. As Puccini was well aware, *La rondine* was his most fragile offspring, too easily obliterated. Yet the glorious big quartet in Act II was a model of its kind, which Puccini knew exactly how long to spin out, and how to stamp indelibly on an audience's memory. It is a work, as Opera North demonstrated, whose time has come, but that does not make its style any easier to capture satisfactorily.

6

*Cover design for the Ricordi
edition of Turandot, in the
'Liberty Style' which the
publishers favoured for all
of Puccini's operas*

*My opera will be given incomplete, and then
someone will come on the stage and say to the
public, 'At this point the composer died.'*

Giacomo Puccini, in anticipation
of the first night of *Turandot*

The Last Years 1917–24

Composing *La rondine* for an enemy power must have been frustrating for Puccini, who invariably put music before politics, but it was obviously not too taxing. The performance Austria finally saw, however, appears to have been hardly worth the wait. By then the composer had completed his revisions, and Adami's Italian libretto had been translated back into German. But Vienna was in no fit state – and perhaps by then had no great desire – to present what it assumed to be a fluffy piece of Franco-Italian escapism to which it had wanted access several years earlier.

According to Puccini – who naturally journeyed to Vienna to inspect it – the performance was mediocre, the scenery looked impoverished, and credibility was challenged by a tenor who sang in Italian while everybody else sang in German (a bad old Teutonic solution to casting problems, and one still practised today). Puccini's response was predictable. 'I am,' he announced to Sybil Seligman, 'going to rewrite *La rondine* for the third time.' Even though that threatened to complicate the issue further, it has continued to leave today's performers with two quite distinctive, and two equally viable, endings to the opera. With all the cunning of a Rossini, Puccini adjusted more or less identical music to suit two quite different dramatic situations. In one of them, Violetta-fashion, the courtesan heroine altruistically walks out on her lover because she fears she might become a burden to him. In the other, Alfredo-fashion, he walks out on her because he is unable to cope with her past.

But even before *La rondine* had first soared at Monte Carlo in 1917, Puccini's attention was beginning to focus on an altogether different operatic idea, to which he had been attracted during his period of enforced wartime travel restriction. For Puccini to find himself at work on two projects simultaneously was unusual to say the least, but then the war had placed him in unusual circumstances. In any case the idea of a triptych of one-act operas that could form a single unit under the title of *Il trittico* had been with him, somewhat dormantly, for many years.

True, the wise Giulio Ricordi (before his death in 1912) had counselled caution. Sets of one-act operas, like collections of short stories, traditionally lack publisher appeal, because they are reckoned to attract a poor box-office return. Such operas might also, as the astute Ricordi recognized, be subsequently prised apart and matched to works by other composers, thus reducing profits. But Puccini was excited enough to visualize the possibility of brilliant contrasts of melodrama, sentiment, and comedy presented as an entity in a single evening, in the manner of French *Grand Guignol.* Showing astonishing decisiveness, he pressed ahead with the scheme. The first of the works, *Il tabarro*, was completed before *La rondine* had its première, which was quite an achievement, and the second, *Suor Angelica*, was already on the stocks.

Happily, Tito Ricordi, by then fully installed as his father's successor, was enthusiastic about a Puccini triple bill and welcomed the opportunity for a reunion with the composer after their *rondine* rift. Indeed, of all Puccini's operatic projects, *Trittico* (Puccini preferred to call it *Il trittico*) proved one of the most trouble-free. This was due at least partly to his beneficial working relationship with his latest librettist, Giuseppe Adami, with whom he enjoyed an uncommonly calm rapport. Twenty years Puccini's junior, Adami was gifted, responsive, and ultimately a friend to whom the composer could confide some of his darkest, most troubled thoughts. After Puccini's death, Adami would write two biographies of him and compile an invaluable collection of his letters.

But Adami was not Puccini's only new young ally. It was the talented Tuscan-born Giovacchino Forzano who, by a remarkable stroke of luck, suggested that *Suor Angelica* and *Gianni Schicchi* – two of his own plots – might form the rest of *Il trittico*, and it was Renato Simoni, Adami's fellow Veronese, who later participated with him on writing the libretto of *Turandot*, Puccini's last opera. The stalwart Illica and Giacosa had been replaced finally, but Puccini, alas, did not live long enough to reap the full harvest of this new collaboration. Yet *Il trittico* and *Turandot* were harvest enough, and they could be said to have rounded off the history of Italian opera, at least so far as large audiences are concerned.

Il tabarro, which served as the launching pad for the rest of *Il trittico*, represented Puccini the Impressionist, with Paris and the River Seine – of which the composer had first-hand knowledge – as its thoroughly appropriate backcloth. Its inspiration was a drama by Didier Gold entitled *La Houppelande* ('The Cloak'), which Puccini had seen and savoured as far back as 1912 on one of his jaunts to France. At that time he earmarked Illica as its obvious librettist, and told him that its subject was *'apache* [i.e., to do with the low life of Paris] in all its meanings'. But in the end it was Adami who adapted the story of this horrific *crime passionel* set on and around a barge moored to a quay in the shadow of Notre Dame.

The story belonged to the grimly naturalistic world of Émile Zola's French novella, *Thérèse Raquin*, and Puccini clearly recognized its links with the 'realistic' tendencies of Italian opera of the period, of which he had already shown awareness – at least in his attention to ambience – in *La bohème, Madama Butterfly* and *Tosca*. The *verismo*, or 'veristic', style undoubtedly had its roots in the more violent side of

Puccini with the Tuscan-born playwright Giovacchino Forzano, librettist of *Suor Angelica* and *Gianni Schicchi*

Verdi, though few of the supporters of Italy's most heroic nineteenth-century composer, who tend to be scathing about his successors, would be prepared to admit it. But Verdi was not its only source. It was equally well a feature of *La gioconda*, composed by Puccini's old teacher, Amilcare Ponchielli, in 1876, and from there it spread rapidly through the music of Mascagni and other composers who wanted to escape from traditional operatic subjects by way of an emphasis on very often squalid behaviour and base emotion.

The trend was not confined to opera, nor indeed to Italy. It influenced drama and literature, too, and some would say debased them. Yet in the period after Italian political unification, it provided rich and useful scope for composers and writers who wished to uphold – or more often perhaps exploit – a sense of regionalism, particularly the peasant regionalism of Mascagni's *Cavalleria rusticana* and Verga's Sicilian story upon which it was based. Although not himself a *verismo* composer in the crude Mascagni sense, Puccini adopted the genre when it suited his purposes, as it definitely did in his vivid depiction of the sights and sounds of Parisian life in *Il tabarro*.

Yet, as in previous works, musical atmosphere was his aim, and he provided it instantly in the impressionistic tints of the muted theme for strings and woodwind with which he sets the Seine in motion in the opening bars. To this he added the sound of a ship's siren, the strains of a stevedore song, the discordant tones of a passing barrel-organ (playing its vinegary little waltz so reminiscent of Stravinsky's *Petrushka*), and a bugle-call from a nearby barracks.

The opera, indeed, is a compendium of allusions. When a ballad-singer wanders along the quay, it is 'The Story of Mimi' (complete with a quotation from *La bohème*) that he sings. When the heroine, Georgetta, nostalgically recalls her trips to the Bois de Boulogne, the horns imitate the call of a cuckoo. When the wife of one of the stevedores sings of her cat, we hear the cat. The work's various motifs – particularly the Debussy-like river one – are constantly employed and developed, in order to build up a musical subtext to the thoughts and actions of the characters. It was a little similar to *Nuages*, the first of Debussy's three orchestral *Nocturnes*, with the addition of people, and it established Puccini, if he was not established already, as one of the greatest orchestrators in a period of great orchestrators.

Opposite, another of
Ricordi's stylized cover
pictures, this time for
Il tabarro; in this the
cloak worn by the jealous
Michele, skipper of a
Seine barge, plays a grue-
some part in the opera's
denouement.
Right, the closing scene of
Il tabarro at its New York
première in 1918, with Luigi
Montesanto as the
triumphant Michele, Claudia
Muzio as Giorgetta, his
wife, and Giulio Crimi as
Luigi, her murdered lover.
Toscanini loathed the *Grand
Guignol* elements of the
work, and offended Puccini
by refusing to conduct it.

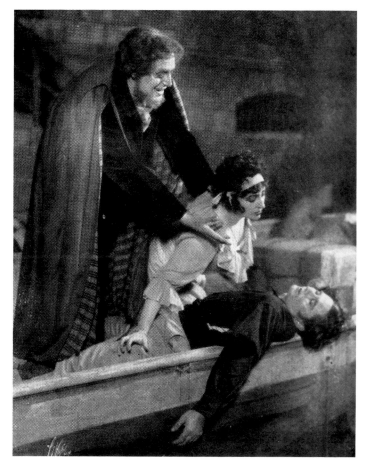

Although he claimed at one point that *Il tabarro* could have
developed into more than a one-act opera, its very brevity – an
element of most *verismo* operas – forms part of its strength. The
structural problems Puccini invariably wrestled with in his longer
works are not an issue here. Nor did they greatly trouble him in
the two other musical panels of his triptych. Before Giovacchino
Forzano offered him *Suor Angelica* – it was originally intended to
be a spoken drama – Puccini had no idea where *Il trittico* was
heading. But the moment this fellow-Tuscan suggested a work set
in a convent with an all-female cast, Puccini knew he was on
his way.

It was a subject, after all, with which he was already acquainted. One of his own sisters was a nun, residing in an Augustinian convent at Vicopelago, near Torre del Lago. Puccini called her 'la mia suorina' ('my little nun') and was clearly fond of her even though, inevitably, they did not meet very often. When he visited her they performed a family ritual whereby he would bring out his wallet and she would remove from it what she needed for convent funds. How much was in the wallet, and how much she felt entitled to take out, were of course another matter. Puccini, even at the height of his fame, was not known for generosity.

Nevertheless, since she was an organist – just as he himself had been in years gone by – he ensured that the convent was equipped with an instrument good enough for her to play. Simonetta Puccini, the composer's granddaughter, has claimed that the convent once actually contained a Suor Angelica, 'who died young'. But even if that sounds too good to be true, Puccini's meetings with his sister – who, being a not unambitious Puccini in her own field, ultimately rose to the level of Mother Superior – enabled him to capture the atmosphere of the place in music just as effectively as he portrayed the River Seine in *Il tabarro*.

Yet poor *Suor Angelica* has long rivalled *La rondine* for the role of the ugly duckling among Puccini's mature operas. Its sentimentality, culminating in a final miracle, has been considered the price that must be paid for the pungency of *Il tabarro* and the mercurial wit of the third opera of the triptych, *Gianni Schicchi*, in which a tiny snippet of Dante about a rich Florentine's bequest, and its effect on his mercenary family, is expanded into a picaresque masterpiece of intrigue and disguise.

Puccini called *Suor Angelica* his 'cloister opera', and it was the one he really cared about. He named it – to the astonishment of some of his critics – the best of the triptych and objected strongly whenever *Gianni Schicchi* was singled out for praise or (worse) for separate performance. He was strongly aware, as he had already shown in *Tosca*, that religion made good theatre; and to verify the 'authenticity' of *Suor Angelica*, while he was at work on it, he sang portions of it to the nuns at his sister's convent, reducing them to tears. Their enthusiastic response was obviously reassuring.

All three works were composed at uncommon speed, and were scheduled to be presented as an entity at the New York Metropolitan in December 1918, with their Italian première to follow early in 1919 in Rome. By a nice conceit, the first of the Metropolitan's performances of the triptych was described as their world première 'on Earth', though destiny forced Puccini to be absent from it. The war in Europe may have been over, but international travel, to the peripatetic composer's chagrin, remained impossible.

His hopes that Toscanini would conduct the first performance were dashed for different reasons. Toscanini, it turned out, loathed *Il tabarro*, dismissing it as *Grand Guignol* of the worst kind, and would have nothing to do with it. His contempt for it caused a temporary rift between him and the composer, during which Puccini referred to his old friend and champion as a 'pig'.

Few other people, indeed, at first recognized *Il trittico* as the beautifully balanced triptych it was intended to be. *Gianni Schicchi*, coming last and brilliantly upstaging the two other works, was all too conspicuously the hit of the evening. Of Puccini's gradual but carefully calculated progress from the nocturnal darkness of *Il tabarro* through the soft glow of *Suor Angelica* to the Florentine radiance of *Gianni Schicchi*, there was simply no awareness. The three works were regarded as separate entities, perfectly interchangeable with other one-act operas by other composers. We shall never know for sure whether Puccini consciously designed *Il trittico* to represent three aspects of Dante. But with *Il tabarro*, *Suor Angelica*, and *Gianni Schicchi* symbolizing *Inferno*, *Purgatorio* and *Paradiso*, the triptych can be seen to possess a further unity, as Mosco Carner has pointed out.

This would also explain why – quite apart from the money aspect – Puccini got so cross when one or another of the three works was performed along with something by another composer (especially if it was a composer he did not like). The Met, after the effect of the première had worn off, teamed *Il tabarro* with Strauss's *Salome* – which, as an evening of domestic mayhem, did actually have some point. But pairing it with Mascagni's *Cavalleria rusticana* or Leoncavallo's *Pagliacci*, as also sometimes happens, has done Puccini no favours.

Rather more appropriate was the Florence Maggio Musicale's coupling in 1969 of *Gianni Schicchi* with Gian Francesco Malipiero's *Sette canzoni* ('Seven Songs'), a mosaic of tiny, sharp-edged, mostly death-conscious music dramas. Dating from 1919, these operatic

Following page, the evocatively Parisian decor for the New York production of *Il tabarro*, suggesting the grim Zola-esque atmosphere of the plot and the impressionism Puccini brought to his music

fragments were of the same vintage as *Schicchi* itself. Moreover, with their hints of Puccini in what could be described as his Debussy and Stravinsky mode, they were not out of keeping with their comic but equally mordant companion-piece.

The trouble with *Il trittico* as a unit is simply that it forms too rich and copious an evening. Each work lasts approximately an hour. Extended with intervals they end up being considerably longer than any of Puccini's full-length operas, which is why opera companies unsympathetic to the fragile beauty of *Suor Angelica* are prone to omit it. Yet patient listeners should have no difficulty coping with this quietest and palest of all Puccini's works, whose inspiration grows almost entirely from the four bell-chimes with which it opens. Puccini, born in a city of bells, was always responsive to their sonorities. If ever he wrote his own Lucca environment into his music it is unquestionably here. The soft Lucchese countryside filled with birdsong is painted by the orchestra (that Puccini would in fact have taken potshots at the birds is beside the point). The sweetness of the nuns' choruses is the antithesis of the miners' music in *La fanciulla del West* and an anticipation of the sound-world of Francis Poulenc's *Les Dialogues des Carmélites* of forty years later.

Yet *Suor Angelica* is not soft-centred. What saves it from any such accusation is the entry, at the very heart of the opera, of the Principessa, Angelica's aunt, who casts a chill over the music before she even utters a word. She is a Turandot who never melts, and is never won, and the very fact that Puccini gave both of them the same royal title (*principessa* means 'princess') suggests that, when he came to compose his last great opera, he was well aware of the similarity between the two women. In *Suor Angelica*, the Principessa brings tidings of disaster for the opera's gentle heroine. Frigidly informing Angelica that her illegitimate son (because of whom she was sent to the convent to repent) has died, she offers no hint of compassion. All Angelica can now contemplate, after her poignant elegy ('Senza Mamma') for her dead child, is suicide, by one of the poisonous flowers she cultivates in the sunny convent garden.

It is clear that Puccini intended the Principessa to be the vindictive opposite of Angelica, just as, in the later opera, Turandot is the ferocious counterpart of the harmless Liù. Whether or not *Suor Angelica* can be called a masterpiece tends to hinge in the end on the

Opposite, the Ricordi cover of Suor Angelica, centrepiece of Il trittico. The nun in the picture was brought to life in the New York première by Geraldine Farrar, famed for the seductiveness of her voice.

question of the plot and its final miracle, whereby Angelica is guided
to Heaven by her dead child. But miracles do not necessarily damn an
opera. It all depends, as usual, on the quality of the composer, and on
one's ability to recognize the difference between, for instance,
something as mawkish as Gian Carlo Menotti's *Amahl and the Night
Visitors* and something as truthful as Britten's *Curlew River*.

In this respect, Puccini's opera is wholly convincing. Miracle or not
– and how easy it is to sneer at the denouement – *Suor Angelica*
sustains its delicate pastoral tone from first note to last,
accommodating without difficulty the intrusion of the Principessa and
the sentiment of the final catharsis. To consider it 'unworthy' of the
rest of the triptych, or as the 'expendable' portion of what could seem
a dauntingly long evening, is to show a failure of trust in Puccini's
impeccable sense of timing.

Of course *Il trittico* adds up to a long evening. That is exactly what
Puccini meant it to do, and why he became annoyed when people
complained. To drop *Suor Angelica*, or to couple *Gianni Schicchi* with
a work by someone else, is simply an example of taking the easy way
out of presenting a demanding triptych the way its composer
intended. And although there have been times when, as a critic with a
deadline to meet, I have cursed Puccini for compiling so lavish an
operatic entertainment, with changes of décor that almost always
entail long intervals, I have invariably been won back by any
production good enough to show how brilliantly Puccini himself rose
to the challenge.

A good production, moreover, confirms that *Gianni Schicchi*, for all
its zest, is not the jewel in *Il trittico*'s crown but simply one of three
equally fine but artfully contrasted gems. That it comes last, that it is
the raciest, and that it contains 'O mio babbino caro' no doubt
explain why people prize it above the other two operas. Puccini
himself knew that it had to seem like the goal towards which the
evening was working. He flung the fleetest music he ever wrote into
this fourteenth-century Florentine imbroglio – his one and only
comedy – about the fate of a family fortune. In this complicated
bedroom farce, the roguish Gianni Schicchi impersonates a rich dying
man in order to distribute the money the way the invalid's family
want it. In the end, he turns the tables on them by ensuring that it is
he himself, and his daughter Lauretta, who benefit. Although by this

The rascally hero, Gianni Schicchi, of the third and most popular of the *Trittico* operas – as seen through the eyes of Ricordi's cover designer

Following page, a scene from the original New York Metropolitan production of *Gianni Schicchi*, with Giuseppe De Luca as the Florentine rogue who, disguised as a dying old man, outwits the greedy relatives who are interested only in the contents of the will

stage in his career Puccini was increasingly accused of having lost his grip, he demonstrated in Lauretta's little aria that he could still turn a melodic line like nobody else.

Indeed, the way the radiant lyricism of 'O mio babbino caro' drifts naturally into this otherwise hyperactive score, then drifts just as naturally out of it again, is an example of Puccini's sleight of hand at its most deft. Yet it is no mere show-stopper. Its appearance so early in the opera (albeit at an important point in the unfurling of the story)

asserts the composer's confidence that the rest of the work is no anti-climax. Nor is 'O mio babbino caro' even sung by the major character. Almost as soon as his daughter Lauretta has sung it, she is sent on to the patio to return only very briefly later in the opera. The work, in fact, is a constellation of brilliant character sketches, each of them enhancing in one way or another the central baritone role of Schicchi himself. As a vehicle, in our own time, for Tito Gobbi, this role has remained one of the highpoints of Italian operatic comedy, a worthy successor to Verdi's Falstaff. Yet it makes its full effect only when it can be perceived to be the logical outcome of Puccini's two preceding one-act operas.

By now it was obvious that Puccini's musical range – always wider than snooty people make it out to be – had widened further since the time of *Tosca* and *Madama Butterfly*. He was sixty years old and one of the most celebrated composers of his day. He was alert to all the musical trends and knew how to turn them to his advantage. And though, in the Wagnerian sense, he had no ambition to change the world, he set his sights with unerring accuracy once he had found the right target upon which to turn them. This, admittedly, took time. His inability to decide on a subject persisted to the end of his career, and his last opera, the unfinished but fortunately not unperformable *Turandot*, cost him as much effort as any other.

His private life, moreover, continued to be disturbed by upheavals of one kind or another long after the pain of the Doria Manfredi episode had receded. It would be easy to suspect that this unhappy episode lay behind his decision, in 1921, to move away from his beloved villa at Torre del Lago, where he had composed the best of his music but where his neighbours would never forget the tragedy Elvira had caused. But to suggest that, in the circumstances, he must have been glad to escape from the scene of the scandal would be to endow Puccini with a sensitivity of a sort that single-minded creative artists seldom seem to possess. As the writer Martin Amis has been quoted as saying, giving birth to your next novel can be more important than saving your marriage.

More to the point, therefore, was the fact that Puccini was being increasingly irritated by the noise and smell of a peat-processing factory that had been installed at Torre del Lago during the war. It was wrecking the calm of his surroundings. Although he battled to have it closed down – one wonders whether his neighbours, some of whom

A photograph of Puccini, prematurely ageing, but as well groomed as ever

worked in it, supported him in his efforts – he was forced to accept defeat and ultimately retreated to a new custom-built villa in the nearby seaside resort of Viareggio, which would be his home until his death three years later.

This elegant, somewhat subdued, low-slung building reflected Puccini's mood of the time. Today, viewed from the street, its façade and veranda possess a faintly oriental air in keeping with a composer who, having produced *Madama Butterfly*, was by then at work on *Turandot.* In the 1920s, it was less hemmed in by loftier buildings than it is now. But there is still parkland with pine trees across the road, and the beach – though hardly a substitute for Puccini's beloved lakeside – is only a few hundred yards away. Today, as business premises, the house excludes casual visitors and is in no sense a memorial to the composer. But the adjoining square has been named the Piazza Giacomo Puccini, and the villa itself continues to exude a private, rather melancholy Puccini-like air. It is easy to visualize Toscanini, his moustache bristling, impatiently pressing the hidden bell that caused the gate to swing open. Easy, too, to imagine the composer's rain machine that sprinkled water from the trees, beneath which he would stand with an open umbrella, cooling himself from the summer heat.

When Norman Douglas, the Italophile author of *South Wind*, visited Viareggio in the very year Puccini moved into his new home,

Puccini's purpose-built villa in Viareggio, to which he moved after the noise of a local peat-processing factory had begun to disturb the peace of his beloved Torre del Lago in the early 1920s

he called it 'a town of heart-rending monotony, the least picturesque of all cities in the peninsula, the least Italian'. But he was being too severe. After Viareggio's timbered sea front and chalets had been destroyed by fire in 1917, handsome 'Liberty-style' villas and hotels replaced them. Puccini's house in the via Buonarroti was thoroughly modish. Not far away, the Gran Caffè Margherita, designed by the distinguished Art Nouveau artist Galileo Chini, must have reminded him of his friend Alfredo Caselli's similarly stylish café in Lucca's main street.

Because, like many other Italians, Puccini believed that property was an excellent form of investment, he had bought land in Viareggio six years before he actually built his villa there. He also prudently held on to his Torre del Lago villa, which was later to become his mausoleum and museum. Much as he loved it, it had never been his sole place of residence. From time to time, his blossoming career had enabled him to acquire other dwellings, including an easily reachable mountain retreat above Chiatri and a summer one at Abitone. He even, as already mentioned, managed to regain his own birthplace on the via del Poggio in Lucca. His sad abandonment of Torre del Lago for Viareggio – 'the greatest sorrow of my life', as he melodramatically remarked to Sybil Seligman – was tempered by his protracted negotiations to acquire a quite different Torre (the Torre della Tagliata in the Tuscan Maremma) to serve as his latest hunting lodge in surroundings said to be teeming with game.

All this, of course, could seem like just another self-created obstacle between him and his next opera, though in fact by then he had largely decided that *Turandot* was to be his subject. Naturally there had been other possibilities, one of them yet another Belasco play, entitled *The Son-Daughter*, which Geraldine Farrar among others had recommended to him. Puccini himself fancied the idea of an opera connected in some way with his hometown of Lucca. Failing to find one (but holding in reserve the opportunity to forge a comic opera out of the prologue to *The Taming of the Shrew*) he switched his attention to a slice of English *verismo*, Dickens's *Oliver Twist*, a dramatization of which he had seen in London in 1919. But not even the opportunity to add Nancy to his gallery of ill-treated heroines could distract him in the end from the manifest appeal of Count Carlo Gozzi's *Turandot*, a subject that came his way via Renato

Simoni, a Milanese drama critic and literary editor almost twenty
years Puccini's junior.

Simoni was enough of a Gozzi scholar to have already written a
drama about the career of the eighteenth-century Venetian playwright.
Although he had known Puccini for some time, and had gone
shooting with him at Torre del Lago (Puccini enticing him there with
the promise of 'some rare beast'), they had never previously worked
together. But now came the opportunity. With the support of
Giuseppe Adami, librettist of *La rondine* and *Il tabarro*, Simoni
suggested that the answer to Puccini's problem might lie in Gozzi's
tragi-comic Chinese fable about the icy princess who posed riddles to
would-be suitors and beheaded them when they answered wrongly, as
they invariably did. Puccini immediately saw its possibilities. Over
lunch with Simoni and Adami in Milan, he agreed to read the play.
Adami, in his eagerness to convince the composer, dashed home to
collect his copy of Schiller's German adaptation of it, back-translated
into Italian. Armed with this, Puccini then set off to attend a
successful revival of *Il trittico* in Rome. After reading it on the train,
he wrote to Simoni saying that they need look no further for a subject.

A 'foreign lady', whom he had encountered in Rome, had told him,
he said, all about Max Reinhardt's famous German production of
Turandot, with incidental music by Ferruccio Busoni. The details
fascinated him. The actress portraying Turandot, he learned, had been
'a tiny, tiny woman, surrounded by very tall men, especially chosen for
their height'. 'Big chairs,' Puccini enthused, 'big furnishings, and this
little viperish woman with a strange hysterical heart.' The idea of
Turandot's hysterical heart seems to have been what clinched the
matter. Perhaps she reminded him of his wife. At any rate, as he put it,
he identified *Turandot* – whose original title, *Turandotte*, confirms that
the final 't' was meant to be enunciated – as 'the most normal and
human play in Gozzi's entire output'. But the plot, he pointed out,
would have to be simplified, and Turandot's amorous passion –
'which has suffocated for so long beneath the ashes of her great pride'
– to be heightened.

Plainly, Puccini sensed that in Simoni and Adami he had found the
right successors to Illica and Giacosa, both of whom were by now
dead ('Poor Illica, another one gone,' he had lamented in December
1919). The old line-up of composer plus two librettists was back in

business in a bright new format, or so it seemed. But as Puccini would soon discover, the old difficulties remained in place, especially when the question of the superhuman final love duet was reached.

Meanwhile he was eager to get down to composing an opera again, especially after the brief, but subsequently embarrassing, diversion that had been provided two years before in the form of an invitation to compose one of his rare concert pieces – a celebratory *Ode to Rome* commemorating the end of World War I. The fact that the normally slow-moving Puccini completed it in less than a week suggests either fierce inspiration or total lack of interest. Puccini's own description of it as 'a real piece of rubbish' supplies the answer. But though he valued it no more highly than Elgar valued *Land of Hope and Glory*, it enjoyed a similar sort of success when it received its open-air première by vast forces at Rome's National Stadium. The public adored it. Mussolini's fascists, about whom Puccini held ambivalent views, soon adopted it. But Puccini, who rightly despised it, fortunately did not live long enough to learn that it had been renamed the 'Hymn to the Duce'. Though he had once been thoughtless enough to describe Mussolini as 'the man we need', it was only in the sense that the things that mattered to Puccini – such as a peaceful existence, trains that could be relied upon, and nothing to impede his foreign travels – were things he thought Mussolini similarly cared about.

Yet he had no one to blame but himself and his vanity for his own awful hymn's existence. The chance to compose it had been provided by Prince Prospero Colonna, mayor of Rome, and Puccini hoped that it would help him to become a Senator of the Kingdom of Italy – an appointment Verdi had held before him, and which Mascagni similarly coveted. This, rather than political status, was clearly the real motive for so irrelevant an ambition. His political acumen had in no way improved since his Austrian misadventure over *La rondine*, but he was not prepared to let his old Italian rival and composer of *Cavalleria rusticana* gain any advantage over him. In the end he got the award he so fatuously desired, then with typical self-mockery described himself as 'sonatore' (i.e., musician or player) rather than 'senatore'.

Nevertheless this did not prevent him asking Sybil Seligman whether, as 'an old man' who had 'reigned over Covent Garden for many years', he might be entitled to receive 'some sort of honour' from King George V. For a sample of the level of political

Benito Mussolini, whose fascists adopted Puccini's *Ode to Rome*, renaming it – without the composer's knowledge – *Hymn to the Duce*

expediency on which Puccini operated, one need look no further
than this.

Meanwhile there was growing evidence in his correspondence of
his fear that time was running out for him. In August 1922, his desire
to seize his opportunities prompted the most extensive of all his motor
trips. In company with his son Tonio (though not Elvira) and some
friends, he set off on an extensive tour of Austria, Germany, and
Holland – he remained cool about France, which, he felt, had never
been sufficiently appreciative of his music. En route, an incident at
Ingolstadt provided him with an unpleasant portent of his mortality.
While lunching on a portion of goose, he almost choked to death on a
bone, thereby damaging his already unhealthy throat. The trip as a
whole, however, was inspirational enough to prompt him to buy
another and even better limousine, this time an eight-cylinder Lancia,
and a new motor-boat that could accelerate to a speed of twenty-five
miles an hour.

But amid such agreeable distractions – including trips to London
and Vienna for further performances of *Il trittico* – he had not
forgotten *Turandot*. Indeed, on the evidence of one of his letters to
Simoni, he was desperate to make progress on it. Reporting himself
to be in a state of 'anxiety, suffering, idleness, and frenzy', he urged
Simoni to get on with the text. Already, he said, he was jotting
down themes, conceiving processions, whispering hidden choruses
to himself, and inventing unearthly harmonies. 'Hurry, hurry,' he
exclaimed. 'I'd like all the work finished, choice, polished.' After
the inanity of the *Hymn to Rome*, he knew that the zeal he would
bring to *Turandot* would confirm his status in the one field that
really mattered to him: that of the leading opera composer of
the day.

Richard Strauss, who was by then at work on his autobiographical
opera, *Intermezzo*, remained his most obvious rival – though his real
rival, if only he had known it, was a then little-known (at least in
Italy) Czech composer, four years older than himself, called Leoš
Janáček. Ever since 1904, in a then neglected opera entitled *Jenůfa*,
Janáček had been showing an uncanny ability to match Puccini's
world-famous dramatic lyricism despite the disadvantages of
composing music in an inaccessible language in the comparative
obscurity of his hometown of Brno.

Leoš Janáček, Puccini's great Czech contemporary, whose operas – *Jenůfa* and *Katya Kabanová* in particular – showed a similar compassion for down-trodden heroines

In the closing pages of *Jenůfa* there is a recurring phrase that is hauntingly reminiscent of *Madama Butterfly*, composed in the same year. Yet neither composer could possibly have known the other's work. Janáček, also, portrayed down-trodden heroines, and he did so with a compassion arguably fiercer and more starkly etched than Puccini's – though Puccini supplied compensation in the form of sheer melodic fertility. It would be hard to imagine Pavarotti singing Janáček.

The parallels between the two composers continued into the 1920s, when Janáček wrote *Katya Kabanová*. The love-lorn heroine of this emotionally charged opera could have been one more of Puccini's suffering victims, and its villainess, Katya's mother-in-law, is the Czech composer's equivalent of the Principessa in *Suor Angelica*. As for *The Makropoulos Case*, composed by Janáček two years after Puccini's death, it contains what is surely the ripest of all roles for an operatic prima donna – the heroine, like Puccini's Tosca, actually *is* a prima donna – to have been written between Puccini's *Turandot* and the present.

The simultaneous burgeoning of Puccini and Janáček, as we now realize, has given twentieth-century opera a rich basis of Italian and Czech lyricism, to which Strauss, in his radiant *Arabella* and *Capriccio* vein, added his German voice. And though Puccini's distaste for the sound of Strauss's music prevented him from speaking praisingly of it, he was surely not wholly averse to the composer of *Ariadne auf Naxos*, whose brilliant evocation of the world of *commedia dell'arte* was matched later by Puccini's own fascinating employment of a trio of *commedia dell'arte* figures in *Turandot*. Romance, comedy, and grotesquerie were the ingredients Puccini demanded from Simoni and Adami, long before the libretto of *Turandot* became a reality. These were also the ingredients of Strauss's *Ariadne auf Naxos*, just as much as of Gozzi's play. A *Turandot* by Richard Strauss, as a successor to *Salome* (or even to *Die Frau ohne Schatten*), would surely have been within the realms of possibility.

Puccini's *Turandot* certainly took him into what, for him, was a thrilling new sound world. As its slashing opening notes make arrestingly clear, he was using the orchestra in an entirely fresh way. The old doctrine that he was a composer who did nothing but repeat himself is here revealed once and for all as manifestly untrue. So, too, is the theory that in this last of his operas he had run out of steam, and that his failure to finish it was due to a combination of diminishing inspiration and a psychological loss of grip.

Puccini was, in fact, more confident about *Turandot* than about any other of his operas. His libretto troubles, though tiresome and time-consuming, seemed no worse than those he had endured with Illica and Giacosa. The three years he spent on advancing the opera to somewhere near completion were no longer than he had taken in the past. Considering that he was by then an ill and dying man, it was remarkable that he got as far as he did.

Despite the days of depression, when as usual he seemed prepared to jettison the whole project, and although he expressed worries that his travels kept taking him away from his librettists, Puccini's mood remained mostly buoyant. And in spite of his health, and his awareness of his age, he exclaimed in a letter to Adami: 'Work as if you were working for a young man of thirty, and I shall do my best.' A few months later, he declared that he was spending between ten and twelve hours a day on the composition of *Turandot*, and was working 'like a Roman slave'.

Puccini would have liked to have been thirty again. His chronic anxieties about his music were matched by increasing hypochondria involving chest pains and a general feeling of malaise. When, ultimately, his smoker's cough developed into something more ominous, it was simply a confirmation of all his fears. But the prospect of declining virility seems equally to have worried this long-term philanderer. In 1923 he wrote to Sybil Seligman saying he had heard about a Viennese surgeon who could rejuvenate his clients with a minor operation. A sixty-seven-year-old South American acquaintance, he told her, had been thus treated and was all the better for it – 'he feels as though he were twenty-five again..... it no longer tires him to walk and his mind is fresh and agile.' Sigmund Freud, undergoing the same operation at the same age, lived for a further sixteen years, in spite of suffering from cancer of the tongue.

But Puccini's priorities concerned his sexual prowess. By 1924, the year of his death, he was planning – quite seriously and explicitly – to consult a Parisian surgeon who specialized in improving the sexuality of ageing men by grafting on to their genitals the reproductive glands of apes. Fortunately, the diabetes from which he had been suffering ever since the time of his car accident prevented him from undergoing so embarrassing an operation.

Meanwhile there was *Turandot*, ever and always *Turandot*. 'Hour by hour, minute by minute, I think of *Turandot*,' he told Adami, 'and all my music I have written up to now seems to me a farce.' His moments of frenetic activity were counterbalanced by moods of despair, when he complained that the work would never be finished, when his librettists were criticized as 'these terrible poets of mine', when inspiration seemed to have dried up wholly and when, on touching the keyboard of his piano, he said that his hands got 'dirty

with dust'. The structure of the opera went through the usual Puccini
processes. The old questions arose. Should it be in two acts or three?
Having proposed a two-act libretto to Adami, he naturally soon
increased it to three, then reverted to two, because for a while he was
eager that nothing should delay the opera's climax 'where love
explodes'. Ultimately, however, he saw the wisdom of increasing it to
three again.

Those who have sought to find parallels between *Turandot* and
Puccini's private life have been provided with plenty, if not too much,
material to go on. From a reference in Mosco Carner's exhaustive
study of the composer to a possible psychological link between the
personality of the tender self-sacrificial Liù and that of the real-life
Doria Manfredi, and similarly between the obsessed Turandot and
Elvira Puccini, people have built up theories about the opera being an
autobiographical psychodrama which for supposedly obvious reasons
Puccini was unable to finish.

The *ne plus ultra* of this unfortunate school of thought was Tony
Palmer's notorious Scottish Opera production of the 1980s in which
the whole action of the opera came second to Palmer's determination
to set the story in Puccini's villa at Torre del Lago, with Liù in
housemaid's costume as Doria Manfredi, Turandot as Elvira, and the
heroic Calaf all too recognizably as the composer himself. The
contortions through which the characters were forced in order to fit
Palmer's concept were enough to convince any member of the
audience once and for all that *Turandot* is no more autobiographical
than *Madama Butterfly* or *Tosca*.

To keep ourselves in touch with the reality of *Turandot*, therefore,
we should remember that Liù, far from being one of the reasons for
the opera's existence, was actually an afterthought. Indeed, as Puccini
made plain, she was principally a device whereby the cruel, selfish
Turandot could be provided with a kind, unselfish opposite. 'Have
you considered well the new conception of the little woman?' he asked
Adami at one point, after the arbitrary inclusion of Liù had been
hanging in the balance. It is clear that until then Liù was not one of
Puccini's major considerations. As his correspondence shows, his main
preoccupations continued to be with the shape of the opera, with
Turandot herself, and with the growing importance of the three
Chinese *commedia dell'arte* characters, Ping, Pang and Pong, to whom

Ping, Pang and Pong, the three Chinese *commedia dell'arte* characters to whom Puccini allotted an increasing amount of music while he was working on *Turandot*. In this scene from the 1961 production at the New York Metropolitan, designed by Cecil Beaton, they are played by Robert Nagy, Charles Anthony and Frank Guarrera.

he allotted an increasing amount of music. So much, then, for Liù being a major source of indecision, or a stumbling block to the progress of the opera.

Puccini's death, rather than any sort of psychological obstacle, was what prevented him from completing the last fifteen minutes of his last masterpiece. Tony Palmer's 'solution' to the musical problem of the denouement – which was to substitute an unauthorized reprise of the end of Act I for Franco Alfano's long-established completion of the score – provided further evidence of the wisdom of leaving well alone. In fact, what Puccini left of *Turandot* was enough for anyone to accept that he had known exactly what he was doing, that there was no hint whatsoever of lost inspiration, and that the Alfano ending – commissioned by the Puccini family after the composer's death – is sufficient to convey his intentions. The history of opera has produced many a third act more indecisive and less satisfactory than this.

Following page, a scene from Scottish Opera's controversial 1984 production of *Turandot*, in which the story was presented in autobiographical terms. Calaf, Turandot and Liù were portrayed as Puccini, Elvira Puccini and the ill-fated maid servant Doria Manfredi.

Like every other work he wrote after *Madama Butterfly*, *Turandot* shows Puccini's determination to stretch – though not overstretch – his own abilities. Its orientalisms, albeit partly derived from a Chinese music box lent to him by a friend in the consular service, were more subtly integrated than those of *Butterfly*. Its orchestral colouring, not least its employment of the dry rattle of xylophone tone, showed new brilliance and finesse. Its ritualistic use of rhythm may have owed something to Stravinsky's *Rite of Spring*, but the fact that it actually

anticipated elements of Stravinsky's *Oedipus Rex* shows that Puccini was no mere copy-cat.

For a work that Puccini was thought to have been incapable of finishing, *Turandot* possesses an extraordinary sureness of touch and a complete command of its material. The dramatic acumen with which he prepares the way for Turandot's entry in Act II, the tension of her central aria, 'In questa reggia', and of the incantatory chilliness of the subsequent riddle scene, never slacken. Nor is his melodic fertility ever in doubt. The vulnerable Liù is portrayed with infinite poignancy, especially in her valedictory aria, 'Tu che di gel sei cinta', the words of which were written by Puccini himself, because his librettists failed to supply them when he needed them. Calaf's 'Nessun dorma' likewise provides proof, in the same unfinished Act III, of Puccini's undiminished inspiration, which enabled him to produce one more example of his ability to cram an aria of memorable ardour into the shortest space of time.

The fact that Puccini never managed to complete what would have been the most triumphant – though certainly not the most tender – of his love duets has always provoked speculation. But the truth was surely not that it steered too close to Puccini's own experience of life – in the Elvira and Doria sense – but that it steered so far from it. Turandot's final yielding to Calaf had nothing to do with reality but everything to do with harsh, abrasive fairy tale. And the fact that it does not ring true on a human level was what, as Puccini discovered, made it so hard for him to write.

Yet it was clearly the icy Turandot, not the warm Liù, by whom he was mesmerized. There is ample evidence to show that it was she who attracted him to Gozzi's play in the first place. By November 1922, indeed, Liù was beginning to get in the way. Having forced her into the opera, Puccini had to get her out of it again. 'I think Liù will have to be sacrificed to some sorrow,' he wrote with cool objectivity to Adami, 'but I don't see how to do this unless we make her die under torture. And why not? Her death could help to soften the heart of the Princess.' These, surely, are the expedient words of an experienced professional opera composer who had reached an awkward corner in the last act of an opera and needed to get round it. He would have been surprised to learn that, in the words of future analysts, the problem was all the fault of Doria Manfredi.

By March 1924, though constantly distracted by his sore throat, he had finished the orchestration of the entire work, apart from the ending, for which he still awaited the text. By September, Toscanini had visited him and – deeply impressed – had gone through the score page by page. Nothing, it was thought, stood in the way of a première of the completed work at La Scala in April 1925, even though Puccini, with uncanny perception, anticipated his own death with the words: 'My opera will be given incomplete, and then someone will come on the stage and say to the public, "At this point the composer died."'

Bearing in mind his state of health, it seems pointless to seek psychological rather than physical reasons for his failure to finish *Turandot*. Yet psychological reasons are exactly what commentators have increasingly sought, arguing not only that *Turandot* was the last incomplete chapter of Puccini's autobiography but that earlier operas contained autobiographical features too. In the case of *La bohème* this was undoubtedly true. But Puccini's operas were not autobiographical in the way that Mahler's symphonies undoubtedly were, and to try to impose a Mahlerish scenario on them, when clearly none was intended, is surely futile.

Just because Puccini employed recurring personality types – the same could be said for Verdi and Wagner – does not mean that he was providing his audiences with meaningful coded portraits of himself, of people he knew or would like to have known. His heroines, weak or strong, were almost invariably women he felt comfortable portraying. As Mosco Carner has explained, a crucial element in Puccini's musical calculations consisted of manœuvring his librettos into a shape that triggered his own creative mechanisms. This, with his recurring demands for what he described as 'some sorrow', was what made his inspiration tick. Because Turandot did not conform to type, he needed Liù to help out.

But between September 1924 and his death in that November, he was preoccupied with something more important to him than the personality of Turandot, and that was the state of his throat. Though he did his best to dismiss his fears that his condition might be serious, he had become a frightened man. His throat had always been his weak point and now, like some Italian *maledizione* or curse, it was about to make him pay the penalty for a lifetime of abuse.

Friends, among whom Sybil Seligman was instinctively the first, had begun to realize that he was really ill. Puccini himself secretly consulted a number of doctors who tried to set his mind at rest, but a specialist in Florence uncovered the truth. There was a sinister lump beneath his larynx which, after close examination, was diagnosed as incurably malignant. The information, communicated to Tonio, was withheld from Puccini himself, who was considered to be already too panic-stricken to accept it. Clutching at straws, Tonio sought further advice and discovered that a certain Dr Ledoux in Brussels, through the use of new-fangled X-rays, might be able to halt the progress of the cancer. Puccini, who had already shown his belief in the powers of foreign doctors, set off immediately by train, accompanied by Tonio, and with his sketches for the end of *Turandot* in his suitcase.

The details of his treatment are depressingly well documented. First came a week of X-rays and the placing of a collar round his throat, which made him feel, he said, 'crucified like Christ', but did not prevent him attending a performance of *Madama Butterfly* at the Théâtre de la Monnaie. But worse was to follow. Informed that a hole was to be made in his neck, through which he would be enabled to breathe via a 'rubber or silver' tube, he exclaimed operatically 'My God, what horror!' He was scarcely reassured when, each morning, he found himself spitting 'mouthfuls of dark blood'.

With concern for his diabetic condition and the state of his heart, it was decided that his operation would take place under local anaesthetic. For a man already terrified, this must have been a hideous ordeal. On Monday 24 November, seven radioactive crystal needles were slowly inserted in or around the tumour in his throat. The process took almost four hours, and at the end of it the composer jotted on a note pad: 'I feel as if I have bayonets in my throat. They have massacred me.'

The plan was to leave the needles in position until the following Sunday, then remove them and see what happened. For four days, word travelled the world that he was recovering. He was at least holding his own. But on the evening of Friday 28 November, he suffered a sudden heart attack. For ten hours, still conscious, he clung to life, but died the following morning after receiving the last sacrament. According to Mosco Carner, Dr Ledoux was so upset that he knocked down and killed a pedestrian while driving home in his car.

Puccini's funeral – looking uncannily like Verdi's – progressing through the streets of Milan in the winter of 1924

On Monday 1 December, there was a funeral service in Brussels. Then Puccini's embalmed body was returned by train to Italy, where two days later a second service was held at Milan Cathedral, attended by an enormous crowd of mourners. It was the biggest funeral of a composer since Verdi's. Toscanini conducted La Scala's orchestra and chorus in the Requiem music from *Edgar*. Hina Spani, the Buenos Aires soprano who was appearing in Milan at that time, sang Fidelia's 'Addio, addio, mio dolce amor' from the same opera. Clearly, the music of *Edgar* carried more weight in 1924 than it does now.

Thereafter Puccini's body was transported through a thunderstorm of the sort that has dramatized more than one great composer's death, and temporarily deposited in the Toscanini family vault in Milan's Monumental Cemetery. Mussolini, seizing his advantage, publicly announced that 'this renowned musician' had recently joined the National Fascist Party – though in fact, on their few meetings, Puccini had been greatly intimidated by the dictator, and had discussed only what he hoped might be culturally creative aspects of fascist philosophy. Two years later the coffin was taken to

Torre del Lago, where a mausoleum had been built for it within the Villa Puccini.

Although Puccini himself had made no proposals for his burial – he was hardly the sort of man to tempt providence in that way – it had been suggested to Elvira that Torre del Lago would be her husband's logical resting place. Permission was granted to build a tomb within the villa. When Elvira herself died ten years later, her body was placed beside Puccini's, and since 1946 Tonio, too, has rested there.

But in December 1924, after the bells of Milan had ceased tolling, Puccini's survivors had still to decide what to do about *Turandot*. The composer had died hoping that, even in Brussels, he might be able to continue work on it. Toscanini, a man of decision if ever there was one, now took control. His first action was sensibly to postpone the première for a year. Having already examined the score – and even the unfinished sketches – with Puccini, he knew better than anyone else what was required, and is said to have named Riccardo Zandonai, a Puccini disciple and composer of a *Romeo and Juliet* opera, as the right person for the delicate task of producing a completion of the final scene. But Tonio feared Zandonai to be too talented, and in the end Franco Alfano, the mediocre composer of an opera based on Tolstoy's *Resurrection*, was chosen in the belief that he would not attempt to steal Puccini's thunder. Alfano was certainly no Puccini and, at the age of forty-nine, never would be. But within six months, he had efficiently completed *Turandot*. It was through no fault of his that a disgruntled Toscanini tampered so damagingly with his efforts.

Quite understandably, the conductor wanted the opera to contain as little as possible that was not authentic Puccini. But the cuts he made in Alfano's ending were of the sort whereby impatient conductors traditionally mutilate long works in the interests of brevity. Unfair to Alfano, the alterations were also unfair to Puccini, and were still in force years after Alfano's death in 1954 and Toscanini's in 1957. Only recently has the great conductor's wisdom been actively questioned and a move made to restore Alfano's original completion. But the power still wielded by the House of Ricordi over the ending of *Turandot* was made quite clear when, as already mentioned, Scottish Opera opted for a third solution, which was to discard Alfano entirely and end the opera with a reprise of the musical climax of Act I,

Two of the brilliant costumes
by Brunelleschi for the
posthumous première of
Turandot, conducted by
Toscanini at La Scala

presented with different action. At a late stage in rehearsals, the
company learned that this was not permissible. The different
ending could be performed only if the Alfano were performed as
well. The result was the only occasion in history when *Turandot*
ended twice – first, fully staged, with the music from Act I, and
then, after a pause, with a concert performance by different singers
of the Alfano version.

For audiences, no doubt, the choice of endings remains a
musicological nicety rather than a matter of dramatic importance. So
long as they have the opportunity to hear a Placido Domingo and a
Birgit Nilsson singing at each other as if they were an Italian Siegfried

An autographed picture of the Polish–American soprano, Rosa Raisa, first of a distinguished line of dramatic sopranos to tackle the daunting role of Turandot

and Brünnhilde, they are generally well satisfied with the shorter of the Alfano versions, not least because it incorporates (as Puccini himself desired) a sonorous repeat of 'Nessun dorma'.

The chance to hear even that version, however, was denied those who attended the première at La Scala on 25 April 1926, for that was when, in one of the most famous of all conductor's interventions, Toscanini halted the performance after the death of Liù, laid down his baton, and – confirming the composer's own prophecy – emotionally informed his listeners that 'Here, at this point, Giacomo Puccini broke off his work.' Not until the second performance, two nights later, was Alfano's completion, or at least the portion of it approved by Toscanini, allowed to be heard in public.

Though *The Times*, thundering from London, accused the conductor of 'censorship', the performance as a whole was more favourably received in Milan than any of Puccini's previous operas. The cast included the Polish-American dramatic soprano, Rosa Raisa, who clearly possessed what have been described as the 'lungs of leather and vocal chords of steel' required by the title-role, though Puccini himself had wanted the more glamorous Maria Jeritza, with her peerless upper register, for the part. Miguel Fleta, Domingo's ardent Spanish predecessor, was the heroic-voiced Calaf (Toscanini, it is said, had favoured the sweeter-toned but diminutive Beniamino Gigli) and Maria Zamboni, a celebrated Manon Lescaut – a role she was eventually to record – sang Liù.

The first city outside Italy to stage *Turandot* was Buenos Aires, which seemed only fitting, since the Teatro Colón had championed Puccini's music for much of his career. Vienna (with Lotte Lehmann in the title-role), New York (with Jeritza), and Covent Garden (where an initial series of sopranos were soon to be spectacularly trumped by the young Eva Turner) quickly followed. It was by then apparent that Puccini's last opera demanded, and deserved, nothing less than the most splendid of singers. More recent exponents of the title-role have included Joan Sutherland, Maria Callas, Birgit Nilsson, Katia Ricciarelli, Gwyneth Jones, and Eva Marton.

How, in opera after opera, did Puccini do it? 'Find a good song, and then build an opera around it,' was the advice of Umberto Giordano, Puccini's by no means negligible contemporary, to aspiring Italian composers. There is no doubt that Puccini profited from the example of Giordano's *Andrea Chénier* when, around the time of that opera's brief triumph, he set to work on his own not dissimilar *Tosca*. Puccini had no difficulty finding good songs, which he could pluck from the air more easily than he shot birds. But as *Andrea Chénier* – for which Giordano employed Puccini's own favourite librettist, Luigi Illica – all too disappointingly demonstrates, there is more to a good opera than a good song. Puccini knew it, and increasingly acted on it until, in *Turandot*, he showed that he was in the process of completely renovating his style through the addition of what, for him, was a brave new world of sonority.

The young Eva Turner,
Britain's most famous
Turandot, who surpassed
Rosa Raisa in Italy and
spectacularly trumped
several other exponents of
the role in Covent Garden

If it is a stamp of a composer's genius – as Haydn, Beethoven, and Stravinsky surely proved – that he can move on from a previous success to something entirely and conspicuously different, then Puccini in his maturity had that stamp. Where he would have progressed from *Turandot* we shall never know, though shortly before his death a story set in eighteenth-century Venice was being discussed with Adami. 'Will there be some sorrow in it?' he had characteristically asked the librettist. 'At least a scene to make one weep?'

As his operatic swansong, *Turandot* showed that he still had plenty to say, and was seeking ever more potent ways of expressing it. Whether or not – as Sir Jack Westrup, Professor of Music at Oxford University, persistently claimed – Puccini brought the history of opera effectively to its close is no longer greatly relevant. There are more recent composers, Britten in particular, about whom similar claims could be made. There are others, such as Gian Carlo Menotti and Andrew Lloyd Webber, who have been hailed optimistically as 'the Puccini of our day', or 'the new Puccini', but who are clearly nothing of the kind.

Menotti has fluency and the ability to hit on a striking theatrical idea – both good Puccinian attributes – but reveals at best accomplishment, at worst meretriciousness, where strokes of genius are called for. Webber is popular, but his works, compared with Puccini's, are sorry stuff, melodically insipid and maladroit in their handling of the linking passages which, in the hands of a great composer, are invariably meaningful, scrupulously timed, and form part of a work's master plan. In Webber's case, without genius at the helm, such passages are all too conspicuously the troughs between what purport to be the peaks.

With the passing of time, *Turandot*, then, has come to seem more and more to be the last of a very special line. In the land where opera was born, it is the last Italian opera to remain firmly in the international repertoire. It is a masterpiece that speaks for itself, and for the man who wrote it. That, in the end, is what matters, and it is the epitaph for which Puccini hardly dared to hope.

Classified List of Works

'fp' denotes first public performance, details of which are given where known.

Opera

Le villi ('The Spirits'), opera-ballet in one act, libretto by Ferdinando Fontana after the story *Les Willis* by Alphonse Karr (1883, revised in two acts 1884). fp Milan, 31 May 1884; Turin, 26 December 1884 (revised version)

Edgar, opera in four acts, libretto by Fontana after the verse play *La Coupe et les Lèvres* by Alfred de Musset (1885–8, revised in three acts 1891–2). fp Milan, 21 April 1889; Ferrara, 28 February 1892 (revised version)

Manon Lescaut, opera in four acts, libretto by Luigi Illica, Giuseppe Giacosa, Marco Prago and Domenico Oliva after the novel *L'Histoire du Chevalier des Grieux et de Manon Lescaut* by Abbé Prévost (1889–92). fp Turin, 1 February 1893

La bohème ('Bohemian Life'), opera in four scenes, libretto by Illica and Giacosa after Henri Murger's novel *Scènes de la vie de bohème* (1893–5). fp Turin, 1 February 1896

Tosca, opera in three acts, libretto by Illica and Giacosa after Victorien Sardou's play *La Tosca* (1896–9). fp Rome, 14 January 1900

Madama Butterfly, opera in three acts, libretto by Illica and Giacosa after David Belasco's play *Madam Butterfly* based on John Luther Long's magazine story (1901–3, revised 1904–6). fp Milan, 17 February 1904; Brescia, 28 May 1904 (revised version in two acts); London, 10 July 1905 (2nd revised version in two acts); Paris, 28 December 1906 (revised version in three acts)

La fanciulla del West ('The Girl of the Golden West'), opera in three acts, libretto by Guelfo Civinini and Carlo Zangarini after David Belasco's play *The Girl of the Golden West* (1908–10). fp New York, 10 December 1910

La rondine ('The Swallow'), lyric comedy in three acts, Italian libretto by Giuseppe Adami based on a German libretto by Alfred Maria Willner and Heinz Reichert (1914–16, revised 1919 and 1920). fp Monte Carlo, 17 March 1917

Il trittico ('Triptych'), three one-act operas:-

Il tabarro ('The Cloak'), libretto by Adami after Didier Gold's play *La Houppelande* (1915–16). fp New York, 14 December 1918

Suor Angelica ('Sister Angelica'), libretto by Giovacchino Forzano (1917). fp New York, 14 December 1918

Gianni Schicchi, libretto by Forzano after an episode from Dante's *Inferno* (1917–18). fp New York, 14 December 1918

Turandot, opera in three acts, libretto by Adami and Renato Simoni after Gozzi's play (1920–24), completed by Franco Alfano 1925–26. fp Milan, 15 April 1926

Choral and Church Music

I figli d'Italia bella, cantata for solo voices and orchestra (1877)

Vexilla Regis prodeunt, for two voices or two-part men's chorus and organ (1878)

Motet, Credo, in honour of San Paolino (1878). fp Lucca, 12 July 1878

Messa di Gloria, for four voices and orchestra (1880)

Cantata a Giove (1897)

Requiem, for mixed voices and organ or harmonium (1905)

Orchestral Music

Preludio Sinfonico (1876)

Capriccio Sinfonico (1883), arranged for piano four hands in 1884. fp Milan, 14 July 1883

Scossa elettrica, march, 1896

Chamber Music

Scherzo, for string quartet (c. 1880–83)

String Quartet in D major (c. 1880–83)

Fugues, for string quartet (1882–3)

La sconsolata, for violin and piano (1883)

Three Minuets for string quartet (1890, Nos. 1 and 3 revised and published in 1898)

Crisantemi, for string quartet (1890)

Songs

Puccini did not write many songs and those that have survived are of minor importance. What makes some of them interesting, however, is that he worked material from them into his operas. 'Sole e amore' ('Sun and Love'), for instance, reappears very recognizably in Act III of *La bohème.* 'Mentia l'avviso' ('The Warning was False') is quoted in the tenor aria, 'Donna non vidi mai', for Des Grieux in Act I of *Manon Lescaut,* and the music of 'Morire?' ('To Die?') was incorporated in the second version of Act I of *La rondine* before being deleted from the third version.

'A te', anonymous text (undated but probably a student composition)

'Melanconia', text by A. Ghislanzoni (1881)

'Alor ch'io sarò morto', text by A. Ghislanzoni (1881)

'Spirto gentil', text by A. Ghislanzoni (1882)

'Noi leggeramo', text by A. Ghislanzoni (1882)

'Storiella d'amore', text by A. Ghislanzoni (1882)

'Salve Regina', text by A. Ghislanzoni (1882)

'Ad una morta!', text by A. Ghislanzoni (1882)

'Mentia l'avviso', recitative and aria, text by F. Romani (1883)

'Solfeggi' (1888)

'Sole e amore', text probably by Giacomo Puccini (1888)

'Avanti Urania!', text by R. Fucini (1896)

'Inno a Diana', text by C. Abeniacar (1897)

'É l'uccellino', text by R. Fucini (1899)

'Terra e mare', text by E. Panzacchi (1902)

'Canto d'anime', text by L. Illica (1904)

'Morire?', text by Adami (1917)

'Inno a Roma', text by F. Savatori (1919), also in choral version

Further Reading

The following list is confined to books written in English and still in print. Other books of importance on Puccini are published in Italy, but require a knowledge of the Italian language. The first four books listed are ones I found particularly useful in my research for the present book. Mosco Carner's massive study, though it incorporates many musical examples, is by no means daunting to read. It is the fullest and most authoritative guide to Puccini to have been published in our time. The revised and augmented third edition, published after Mosco Carner's death under the supervision of his widow, is especially valuable.

David Kimbell's *Italian Opera* includes a brief but fascinating section on Puccini and his contribution to the history of opera in Italy. *The Puccini Companion*, edited in Italy by William Weaver and Simonetta Puccini, incorporates illuminating and up-to-date essays by a variety of experts on aspects of each of Puccini's operas.

Ashbrook, W. *The Operas of Puccini* (London, Cassell, 1968; 2nd edition, Ithaca, New York, Cornell University Press, 1985)

Ashbrook, W. and Powers, H. *Puccini's Turandot: The End of the Great Tradition* (New Jersey and Oxford, Princeton University Press, 1991)

Carner, M. *Puccini: A Critical Biography* (London, Duckworth, 1958; 2nd edition, 1974; 3rd edition, 1992)

Carner, M. *Tosca* (Cambridge, Cambridge University Press, *Cambridge Opera Handbook* series, 1985)
Greenfield, E. *Puccini: Keeper of the Seal* (London, Arrow Books, 1958)

Groos, A. and Parker, R. *La Bohème* (Cambridge, Cambridge University Press, *Cambridge Opera Handbook* series, 1986)

John, N. (ed.) *La Bohème: Opera Guide* (London, John Calder, 1982; New York, Riverrun Press)

John, N. (ed.) *Madama Butterfly: Opera Guide* (London, John Calder, 1984; New York, Riverrun Press)

John, N. (ed.) *Tosca: Opera Guide* (London, John Calder, 1982; New York, Riverrun Press)

Kaye, M. *The Unknown Puccini* (New York, Oxford University Press, 1985).

Kerman, J. *Opera as Drama* (New York, Alfred A. Knopf, 1956; revised edition, University of California Press, 1988; London, Faber & Faber, 1989)

Kimbell, D. *Italian Opera* (Cambridge, Cambridge University Press, 1991)

Marek, G. *Puccini: A Biography* (New York, 1951)

Osborne, C. *The Complete Operas of Puccini* (London, Gollancz, 1981)

Weaver, W. and Puccini, S. *The Puccini Companion* (New York and London, W. W. Norton, 1994)

Selective Discography

Puccini was one of the first composers to benefit during his lifetime from the invention of the gramophone. His operatic arias were of a duration that tended to fit comfortably on to one side of a single ten-inch or twelve-inch 78rpm disc, although to accuse him – as some people cynically have done – of crudely exploiting the commercial possibilities of the recording industry seems extremely unfair on a composer who actually believed in brevity.

The voices of many singers for whom Puccini wrote his operas, or about whom he especially cared, are preserved on disc and can often be tracked down on excellent modern transfers. All Puccini's operas have been recorded, the more popular ones many times. Among complete recordings, the historic 1938 *Bohème* and *Tosca*, and the 1940 *Madama Butterfly*, each of them with Beniamino Gigli as tenor, are collector's items.

So, too, are Renata Tebaldi's 1951 recordings of *Bohème*, *Tosca* and *Madama Butterfly*, dating from the earliest days of LP, but still sounding remarkably atmospheric, and wonderfully vocally youthful, in their CD transfers. Alberto Erede's perceptive, purposeful conducting of the Orchestra of the Santa Cecilia Academy, Rome, is another asset of these early Decca sets, just as Herbert von Karajan's more glamorous but no less responsive conducting of the Vienna and Berlin Philharmonics in the same works – with Mirella Freni as Mimi and Butterfly, and Katia Ricciarelli as Tosca respectively – dominates a more recent period in recording history.

All these are performances worth possessing. But the best of all Puccini recordings, and ones which are really essential to any collection of his works, are the 1957 Beecham *Bohème*, with Victoria de los Angeles and Jussi Björling as Mimi and Rodolfo; the 1953 Victor de Sabata *Tosca*, with Maria Callas, Giuseppe di Stefano,

and Tito Gobbi as its vocal triumvirate; the 1966 Barbirolli *Madama Butterfly*, with Renata Scotto and Carlo Bergonzi; and the Rome Opera *Trittico*, recorded between 1956 and 1958 under different conductors (including Tullio Serafin), with Victoria de los Angeles and Tito Gobbi in major roles.

The fact that these performances date from as long ago as the 1950s and 1960s speaks for itself. For all the technical advances in the recording industry, great Puccini singing and conducting has not kept pace with progress. Few of the many performances recorded exclusively for CD can be recommended without reservation. The following list, therefore, must be taken with a pinch of salt. Although it represents, in my view, the cream of what is now available, only the recordings marked with an asterisk may be considered truly outstanding.

Opera

Le villi
Renata Scotto, Placido Domingo, Leo Nucci, Tito Gobbi, Ambrosian Opera Chorus, National Philharmonic Orchestra conducted by Lorin Maazel
SONY MK 76890

Edgar
Renata Scotto, Carlo Bergonzi, Gwendolyn Killebrew, Schola Cantorum of New York, Opera Orchestra of New York conducted by Eve Queler
CBS MASTERWORKS 79213

Manon Lescaut
Mirella Freni, Luciano Pavarotti, Dwayne Croft, Giuseppe Taddei, Chorus and Orchestra of the New York Metropolitan Opera conducted by James Levine
DECCA 440 220-2DH02

* La bohème
Victoria de los Angeles, Jussi Björling, Robert Merrill, Lucine Amara, John Reardon, Giorgio Tozzi, RCA Victor Chorus and Orchestra conducted by Sir Thomas Beecham
EMI CDS7 47235-8

Tosca
Maria Callas, Giuseppe di Stefano, Tito Gobbi, Franco
Calabrese, Angelo Mercuriali, Chorus and Orchestra of
La Scala, Milan conducted by Victor de Sabata
EMI CDS7 47175-8

Madama Butterfly
Renata Scotto, Carlo Bergonzi, Rolando Panerai, Anna
Di Stasio, Piero de Palma, Giuseppe Morresi, Paulo
Montarsolo, Chorus and Orchestra of the Rome Opera
House conducted by Sir John Barbirolli
EMI CMS7 69654-2

La fanciulla del West
Carol Neblett, Placido Domingo, Sherrill Milnes,
Francis Egerton, Robert Lloyd, Gwynne Howell,
Chorus and Orchestra of the Royal Opera House,
Covent Garden conducted by Zubin Mehta
DEUTSCHE GRAMMOPHON 419 640-2GH2

La rondine
Kiri Te Kanawa, Placido Domingo, Mariana Nicolesco,
David Rendall, Leo Nucci, Lillian Watson, Gillian
Knight, Ambrosian Opera Chorus, London Symphony
Orchestra conducted by Lorin Maazel
CBS M2K 37852

Il trittico
Il tabarro
Tito Gobbi, Margaret Mas, Giacinto Prandelli, Piero
De Palma, Plinio Cabassi, Miriam Pirazzini, Chorus
and Orchestra of the Rome Opera House conducted by
Vincenzo Bellezza

Suor Angelica
Victoria de los Angeles, Fedora Barbieri, Mina Doro,
Corinna Vozza, Chorus and Orchestra of the Rome
Opera House conducted by Tullio Serafin

Gianni Schicchi
Tito Gobbi, Victoria de los Angeles, Anna Maria
Canali, Carlo del Monte, Orchestra of the Rome Opera
House conducted by Gabriele Santini
EMI CLASSICS CMS7 64165-2

Turandot
Katia Ricciarelli, Placido Domingo, Barbara Hendricks,
Ruggero Raimondi, Piero De Palma, Gottfried Hornik,
Heinz Zednik, Francisco Araiza, Vienna State Opera
Chorus and Vienna Philharmonic conducted by
Herbert von Karajan
DEUTSCHE GRAMMOPHON 423 855-2

Choral

Messa da Gloria
José Carreras, Hermann Prey, Ambrosian Singers,
Philharmonia Orchestra conducted by
Claudio Scimone
ERATO-WARNER 2295 45197-2

Orchestral

Capriccio Sinfonico
Crisantemi
Minuets Nos. 1–3
Preludio Sinfonico
Edgar (preludes to Acts I and III)
Le villi (prelude and *La tregenda* from Act II)
Berlin Radio Symphony Orchestra conducted by
Riccardo Chailly
DECCA 444 154-2

Chamber

Crisantemi
Alberni Quartet; with quartets by Donizetti and Verdi
CRD CRD 3366

Songs

The Unknown Puccini
Placido Domingo, Justino Diaz, Julius Rudel
SONY SK 44981

Index

Page numbers in italics refer to
picture captions.

Photographic Acknowledgements

The publishers would like to thank Signora Simonetta Puccini for her help with illustrations for this book.

Camera Press, London: 164, 181
Casa Ricordi, Milan: 42, 122
Jean-Loup Charmet, Paris: 120,
  130, 154–5, 223
Deutsche Oper, Berlin: 89, 90–91
Fondazione Puccini, Milan: 18, 26,
  87, 221
The Hulton Getty Picture
  Collection Ltd, London: 30,
  58–9, 209
The Lebrecht Collection: 33, 34,
  69, 73, 93, 138–9
Louis Mélançon (Opera News): 215
Mansell Collection, London: 76–7,
  226–7
Metropolitan Opera Archives, New
  York: 162
Museo Teatrale alla Scala, Milan:
  46–7, 62, 105
Opera North, Leeds: 175
Popperfoto, Northampton: 68
©Robert Selkowitz: 21, 41, 65,
  100–1, 131, 132–3